AMERICAN FE
SERIAL KILLERS

THE FULL ENCYCLOPEDIA
OF AMERICAN FEMALE SERIAL KILLERS

INTRODUCTION

America has a long and complicated fascination with serial killers. When we think about the most infamous of these killers, we generally think of men like Ted Bundy, Jeffrey Dahmer, or John Wayne Gacy. Those names make headlines while there's the often repeated myth that suggests there are no female serial killers. After all, most of us couldn't name a woman on the same scale of infamy at BTK or the elusive Zodiac Killer, can we? As it so often is, the truth is far more complicated.

Women kill. While they are less sensationalized than their male counterparts, they are no less deadly. At time of publication, current research shows that one in six serial killers are female, bringing their number to fifteen percent of confirmed serial killers.

That brings one important question – what defines a serial killer? What makes them different from anyone who takes someone else's life? The FBI definition is succinct: a serial killer is someone who commits at least three murders over more than a month with an emotional "cooling off period" between those murders. That definition seems incomplete, leading many to apply a sense of sexual deviancy to the killing (as in Bundy or Dahmer). While that is common in male serial killers, it only rarely applies to their female counterparts. Most often, their motivations are linked to psychopathic traits and histories of childhood abuse. In other cases, they are more likely to be motivated by profit or revenge. Whatever their motivations, all the women in this encyclopedia are still classified as serial killers.

The Encyclopedia of Female American Serial Killers brings together a collection of the worst of these atrocities and the women behind them. Committed to facts without sensationalism, this book offers a frank, educational look at their crimes. Within the pages of this encyclopedia, you'll find the stories behind some of the deadliest women in American history. This reference book includes background information on the killers, their victims, methods, and – where relevant – their arrests, trials, and convictions. This reference is designed to provide you with the best A–Z guide for a concise, comprehensive databank.

CONTENTS

AMY ARCHER-GILLIGAN 5

VELMA BARFIELD 8

CLEMENTINE BARNABET 10

MARTHA BECK 13

ELVIRA AND KATE BENDER 15

DEBRA BROWN 20

JUDY BUENOANO 23

CAROL MARY BUNDY 26

PATTY CANNON 28

SUZAN BEAR CARSON 30

MARY CLEMENT 32

CYNTHIA COFFMAN 34

FAYE COPELAND 36

MARY FRANCES CREIGHTON 38

NANNIE DOSS 40

CHRISTINE FALLING 42

LAVINIA FISHER 44

CHARLENE GALLEGO 46

JANIE LOU GIBBS 48

BERTHA GIFFORD 50

KRISTEN GILBERT 52

HELEN GOLAY AND OLGA RUTTERSCHMIDT 54

GWENDOLYN GRAHAM AND CATHY WOOD 56

DANA SUE GRAY 58

BELLE GUNNESS 61

ANNA MARIE HAHN 63

LIZZIE HALLIDAY 65

LINDA HAZZARD 67

AUDREY MARIE HILLEY 69

WANETA HOYT 72

MARTHA ANN JOHNSON 74

GENENE JONES 76

SANTE KIMES 78

SHARON KINNE 81

TILLIE KLIMEK 85

THERESA KNORR 87

MICHELLE KNOTEK 89

SHEILA LABARRE 91

DELPHINE LALAURIE 93

RHONDA BELLE MARTIN 96

KIMBERLY MCCARTHY	98
BLANCHE TAYLOR MOORE	100
JUDITH ANN ADAMS NEELLEY	103
MARIE NOE	105
DIANE O'DELL	107
LOUISE PEETE	109
DOROTHEA PUENTE	111
TERRI RACHALS	114
KIMBERLY CLARK SAENZ	116
LYDIA SHERMAN	118
LYDA SOUTHARD	120
GEORGIA TANN	122
MARYBETH TINNING	125
JANE TOPPAN	129
LOUISE VERMILYA	131
SARAH WHITELING	134
SHIRLEY WINTERS	136
MARTHA WISE	138
AILEEN WUORNOS	141

COPYRIGHT © 2019
BY KOLME KORKEUDET OY.
ALL RIGHTS RESERVED.

No part of this book may be reproduced in any form or by any electronic or mechanical means, including information storage and retrieval systems, without written permission from the author, except for the use of brief quotations in a book review.

AMY ARCHER-GILLIGAN

- ◊ **Date of birth:** October 1873
- ◊ **Nickname:** Sister
- ◊ **Motive:** Life insurance money
- ◊ **Number of victims:** 10-50
- ◊ **Date of murders:** 1910 - 1917
- ◊ **Date of arrest:** 1917
- ◊ **Murder method:** Poisoning
- ◊ **Known victims:** Her second husband, Michael Gilligan; clients of her nursing home: Franklin R. Andrews was among them.
- ◊ **Crime location:** Windsor, Connecticut.
- ◊ **Status:** Sentenced to life imprisonment.

BACKGROUND

Amy Duggan, born in October 1868, was James Duggan and Mary Kennedy's daughter. She was born in Milton, Connecticut, and was the eighth of ten children. In 1890 she attended the New Britain Normal School and the Milton School.

In 1897, Amy E. Duggan married James Archer. In December 1897, their daughter, Mary J. Archer, was born. In 1901 Amy and James first became caretakers, hired to take care of John Seymour, who was an elderly widower. They moved into his home in Newington, Connecticut. In 1904, John died. His heirs turned that place into a boarding house for older adults, and the Archers stayed to take care of the elderly for money. They paid rent to Seymour's family. They managed the boarding house called Sister Amy's Nursing Home for the Elderly.

The Archers moved to Windsor, Connecticut, after Seymour's heirs decided to sell the house in 1907. They used their savings to purchase their house on Prospect Street in Windsor Center. The Archers soon turned it into a business called Archer Home for the Elderly and Infirm.

In 1910, James Archer died, probably of natural causes. Bright's disease was the official cause of his death. A few weeks before his death, Amy Archer had taken out an insurance policy on him. The policy benefit permitted her to continue running the Archer Home.

In 1913 Amy married a widower Michael W. Gilligan who had four adult sons. He was wealthy and interested in investing in Amy and the Archer

Home. Nevertheless, on February 20, 1914, Michael died only three months after marrying Amy. Severe indigestion was the official cause of his death. Amy was again financially secure. Her new husband drew a will during their marriage. The testament said that his entire estate belonged to her. Later, the will would be determined to be a forgery as it was written in handwriting matching Amy Archer-Gilligan.

MURDERS

Sixty deaths happened in the Archer Home between 1907 and 1917. Her clients' family members grew suspicious as they counted the many deaths. Between 1907 and 1910, only 12 clients died, but 48 residents died between 1911 and 1916. A healthy man, Franklin R. Andrews, was among them. Andrews was gardening in the Archer house on the morning of May 29, 1914. His strong physical condition deteriorated in a single day, and he was dead by evening. A gastric ulcer was the official cause of death.

Andrews' siblings (Nellie Pierce was among them) found some of his letters and marked cases where Archer-Gilligan was pressing Franklin for money. Not long after giving Amy a large sum of money, her clients died.

As the deaths continued, Nellie Pierce informed the local district prosecutor about her suspicions, but he ignored her. So, she brought her story to The Hartford Courant. The first article on the "Murder Factory" was published on May 9, 1916. In several months, the police initiated a serious investigation of that case, and it took almost a year to complete the investigation.

The police exhumed the bodies of Gilligan, Andrews, and three other lodgers. It turned out that the cause of death was poisoning, either strychnine or arsenic. City shopkeepers testified that Amy had been purchasing a large volume of arsenic, probably to "kill rats." A look into Gilligan's will established that Amy had forged it.

It appeared that Amy bought the arsenic to kill her patients. Some of the patients and their doctor had signed off to buy it. The police prosecuted Dr. King because evidence was piling up against him, but suspicions were focused back on Amy when someone suggested checking all records of arsenic buying.

When the police found evidence that Amy sent her patients to the drugstore to purchase arsenic, they arrested and convicted her.

ARREST AND TRIAL

The police arrested and tried Archer-Gilligan for murder, initially on five items. Finally, her attorney had success in reducing charges to the killing of Franklin R. Andrews. A jury declared her guilty and Amy was sentenced to death on June 18, 1917.

In 1919, Amy Archer-Gilligan appealed and received a new trial. She pleaded insanity at the trial. Mary Archer witnessed that her mother was addicted to morphine. Archer-Gilligan was again convicted of murder and was sentenced to life imprisonment.

OUTCOME

In 1924, Amy Archer-Gilligan was proclaimed to be insane and was moved to the Connecticut Hospital for the Insane in Middletown where she died on April 23, 1962.

MEDIA – TELEVISION

Amy Archer-Gilligan was mentioned on the police procedure crime drama Criminal Minds, in the season five episode, "The Uncanny Valley."

VELMA BARFIELD

- ◊ **Date of birth:** October 29, 1932
- ◊ **Nickname:** The Black Widow
- ◊ **Motive:** Money
- ◊ **Number of victims:** Six
- ◊ **Date of murders:** April 4, 1969 – February 4, 1978
- ◊ **Date of arrest:** May 13, 1978
- ◊ **Murder method:** Poisoning
- ◊ **Known victims:** Her fiancé, Stuart Taylor and her mother, Lillie Bullard
- ◊ **Crime location:** North Carolina, United States
- ◊ **Status:** Death: execution by lethal injection

BACKGROUND

Velma Barfield was raised near Fayetteville, North Carolina, but she was born in rural South Carolina. Her father was physically violent, and her mother, Lillian Bullard, did not intervene. In 1949 Velma got away by marrying Thomas Burke. They had two children and were happy until Barfield had a hysterectomy and developed back pain. These occasions caused a behavioral change in Barfield and an eventual drug addiction.

Burke started drinking, and Barfield's complaints turned into bitter arguments. In April 1969, after Burke lost consciousness, Barfield and the children went out. When they got back, they found the house burned and Burke dead. Several months later, her home burned down, but she had insured it. Velma Barfield

married a widower, Jennings Barfield in 1970. Jennings died in March 1971, from heart complications. It happened less than one year after their marriage.

Barfield's mother, Lillian Bullard, had symptoms of intense diarrhea, vomiting, and nausea. During Christmas in the same year, her mother suffered the same earlier disease but died in the hospital after some hours in December 1974.

MURDERS

Velma Barfield began working for Dollie Edwards and Bullard Montgomery in 1976. She was caring for the elderly. In January 1977 Montgomery was seriously sick, and he died. On March 1, Dollie developed the same symptoms as Bullard. She died only a month after her husband's death. Barfield later confessed to the latter death. The following year, Barfield took another caregiver job, this time for Record Lee, who was 76 and had broken her leg. In June 1977, Lee's husband, John Henry, began experiencing excruciating pains in his chest and stomach along with diarrhea and vomiting. He died soon afterward, and Velma Barfield later confessed to that murder.

Rowland Stuart Taylor was Barfield's boyfriend and another victim. She had been forging checks on Taylor's account and feared he had discovered it. Barfield mixed an arsenic poison into his tea and beer. In February 1978 he died. An autopsy found arsenic in Taylor's system. Jennings' body was exhumed and found to have traces of arsenic. Barfield was arrested but denied having committed that murder. Although she confessed to the murders of Bullard, Dollie, and John Henry Lee, Barfield was judged and convicted only for Taylor's murder.

Jonathan Byrd is a singer-songwriter and the grandson of Jennings and his first wife. He wrote the song "Velma" and released the album "Wildflowers." This song gives a personal account of the murders and investigation.

ARREST AND TRIAL

As said before, the police arrested Barfield after her fiancé's death. She was a prisoner at Central Prison in Raleigh, North Carolina. The area for her was not designated at that time as Barfield was the only woman under a death sentence. They housed her in an area for escape-prone and mentally ill prisoners.

While on death row, Barfield became a devout, born-again Christian. She spent her last few years ministering to prisoners. Barfield's involvement in Christian ministry was to gain a commutation to life imprisonment. Professor of Psychiatry and an authority on violent behavior, Dorothy Otnow Lewis, claimed that Barfield suffered from a dissociative identity disorder. Professor Lewis witnessed that she had spoken to Barfield's other identity, "Billy." He told her that Velma had been a victim of sexual abuse. He, Billy, had killed her abusers. It didn't persuade the judge. "One of them did it," Lewis cited him as saying. "I don't care which one."

The federal court denied Barfield's appeal; she instructed her attorneys to abandon a further appeal to the U.S. Supreme Court.

OUTCOME

On November 2, 1984, Barfield was executed at Central Prison. Before the execution, she made a statement: "I know that everybody has gone through a lot of pain, all the families connected, and I am sorry, and I want to thank everybody who has been supporting me all these six years." Barfield's last meal was one bag of Cheetos and two 8-ounce glass bottles of Coca-Cola. She was buried in a small, rural North Carolina cemetery near her first husband, Thomas Burke.

CLEMENTINE BARNABET

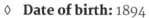

- ◊ **Date of birth:** 1894
- ◊ **Nickname:** Voodoo Priestess
- ◊ **Motive:** Immortality
- ◊ **Number of victims:** 35
- ◊ **Date of murders:** February 1911 – October 1912
- ◊ **Date of arrest:** October 1912
- ◊ **Murder method:** The victims were beaten to death with an ax
- ◊ **Known victims:** Alexandre Andrus, his wife Mimi, his son Joachim aged three years and baby Agnes, eleven months old
- ◊ **Crime location:** Between Lafayette, Louisiana, and Texas
- ◊ **Status:** Sentenced to life but escaped from the prison and was never seen again.

BACKGROUND

An African-American female serial killer, Clementine Barnabet, committed murders in Louisiana and Texas. She was believed to have accomplices as part of a violent religious sect and a cult the "Church of the Sacrifice." In the beginning, her father was under suspicion, but the police investigated her. Barnabet confessed to participation in thirty-five gruesome murders. She was convicted and put into prison for her crimes. Barnabet escaped from jail and was not seen or heard from afterward.

Clementine Barnabet was born around 1894 in St. Martinville, Louisiana and moved to Lafayette, Louisiana in 1909.

Her parents were Nina Porter and Raymond Barnabet. Zepherin Barnabet was her only brother. At the age of 17, Barnabet joined a cult called the "Church of Sacrifice." She started committing the murders while being a member of that cult. Raymond Barnabet was abusive to his family and very aggressive.

The Barnabet murders followed a persistent pattern. Clementine would often kill entire families rather than one person. The crimes were done with an ax. Barnabet cut the heads off of the victims, and once she had butchered the family, she would then lay the bodies in bed together and leave them for police to find them. Barnabet's murders occurred between Lafayette, Louisiana, and Texas.

The first of many murders was committed in February 1911. Walter Byers and his family were murdered.

The police started an investigation to find the killer. The first suspect was Raymond Barnabet, Clementine's father. The Barnabet family witnessed against Raymond and said he had left town that night for unknown reasons and returned home late with blood and brain matter on his shirt and boots. Zepherin, his son, declared that when he came back home, Raymond was boasting about committing murders and said that the family deserved it.

More murders happened during the time police investigated Raymond. The Cassaway family was murdered in March 1911. This caused a shift in the investigation. The mother of the slain family was white, in contrast with the previous two families, which were black. The authorities thought that Raymond committed all three of these mass murders, so the police arrested him and sent him to Lafayette Parish Jail.

Another massacre occurred while Barnabet was awaiting trial. In November 1911, the Randall family was killed like the previous slayings. This raised another suspect and confused the authorities. The police decided to investigate Clementine Barnabet.

MURDERS

On 25 February 1911, on Saturday night, Alexandre Andrus, his wife Mimi, his son Joachim aged three years and baby Agnes, eleven months old, were brutally murdered. It happened in the Trahan and Doucet addition beyond where the railroad tracks cross Vermilion Street.

At 7 am the woman's brother, Lezime Felix discovered that awful crime and called the police. Sheriff Lacoste, deputy Coroner Clark, and other officers at once arrived. A couple and a boy had been brained with an ax while asleep, and the police found the baby, lying in its cradle with its head crushed. The husband and wife were taken up by the killer who placed them on their knees beside the bed. The woman's arm was over the man's shoulder, as if in the attitude of prayer.

The killer entered the house and left through the kitchen door. The crime was committed after midnight; an examination by Dr. Clark disclosed some slight warmth in the bodies.

In the morning, on November 26, 1911, a killer murdered Norbert Randall with his wife, their three children, and a nephew. Their house had three rooms and was situated in Mills addition. A ten-year-old girl, who was the oldest child of the Randall family, discovered the murder. She escaped injury because she was at her uncle's that night. She entered the house through the open kitchen door and found her parents and the children dead in bed, and she called the police. The officers investigated thoroughly. It was a rainy day, so any outside trace of the killer was removed. Nothing inside seemed to have been disturbed. The murder was committed with an ax, which the officers found in the house thoroughly washed.

The murderer struck all victims in the head. The man with his wife and a baby girl were found in one bed and three boys were found in another bed. Sheriff Lacoste arrested Clementine Barnabet.

OUTCOME

What prompted the police to arrest Clementine as the main suspect of many crimes committed in that area? A man's suit covered with blood and brain matter was found in her closet. When arrested, Barnabet rejected all links to the murders.

She, however, admitted to thirty-five murders. Clementine stated that a priestess of the Church of Sacrifice had given her "conjure bags" that would grant supernatural powers and make her undetectable to the authorities. This caused Clementine to commit her first crime to test whether this was true.

In October 1912, Clementine Barnabet, being only eighteen, was sentenced to life in prison at Angola State Penitentiary.

DISAPPEARANCE

Clementine tried to escape jail in July 1913, but the officers caught her before she even made it to the gate. In August 1923, Clementine Barnabet escaped the prison, and nobody saw her again.

MARTHA BECK

- ◊ **Date of birth:** May 6, 1920
- ◊ **Nickname:** The Lonely-Hearts Killer
- ◊ **Motive:** Robberies
- ◊ **Number of victims:** 17
- ◊ **Date of murders:** 1948-1949
- ◊ **Date of arrest:** February 28, 1949
- ◊ **Murder method:** Overdose of drugs, strangulation, shooting, drowning
- ◊ **Known victims:** Myrtle Young; Janet Fay, 66; Delphine Downing, 41, and her two-year-old daughter Rainelle
- ◊ **Crime location:** Illinois, New York, Michigan, USA
- ◊ **Status:** On March 8, 1951, executed by electrocution at Sing Sing prison in New York

BACKGROUND

n May 6, 1920, Martha Beck was born Martha Jule Seabrook in Milton, Florida. She suffered a glandular problem and was overweight. Martha stated that her brother sexually assaulted her because of her early puberty. Her mother did not believe her and beat her, asserting it was Martha's fault.

After school, Martha studied nursing, but had problems getting a job because she was overweight. She became an assistant to an undertaker and prepared bodies for burial. Martha left her job and went to California to work as a nurse in an army hospital. She had promiscuous intercourse and soon became pregnant.

Martha tried to persuade the father of her baby to marry her, but he refused. She returned to Florida, single and pregnant.

Beck told everybody that she had married a serviceman. Later Martha claimed that he died in the Pacific Campaign. The residents of her hometown believed her loss, and the local newspaper published her sad story. Soon she gave birth to a daughter but became pregnant again. The father was a Pensacola bus driver named Alfred Beck. They married quickly but divorced six months after that, and she had a son.

Martha Beck was an unemployed, single mother. She lived in a fantasy world, watching romantic movies and buying romance novels. She found a job at the Pensacola Hospital for Children in 1946. In 1947 she placed a lonely-hearts advertisement in the magazine, and Raymond Fernandez answered it.

MURDERS

Raymond visited Martha and lived with her for a while. Beck told everyone they were getting married. While she prepared for the marriage, he returned to New York. After a while, Martha lost her job and decided to move to New York. She packed up, took her children, and arrived on Fernandez's doorstep. He admitted his criminal business to Beck, who quickly sent her children to the Salvation Army so she could assist Fernandez without obstacles. She posed as his sister, giving him a respectable appearance. Their victims felt more secure in the house, knowing there was another woman there and often accepted invitations to stay with the pair. Martha also assured some victims that she lived alone and that her "brother" was only a visitor. Beck was highly jealous and would go to great lengths to make sure Fernandez and his "targeted" victims never finalized their relationship. When Fernandez had sex with a woman, Beck exposed both to her violent temper.

In 1949 66-year-old Janet Fay became engaged to Fernandez and stayed at his apartment. When Martha caught them in bed, she angrily crushed Fay's head with a hammer. Fernandez then suffocated Fay. Her family became suspicious when Fay disappeared, and Fernandez and Beck ran away.

They went to Wyoming Township, Michigan, where they met Delphine Downing who was young and single and had a two-year-old daughter. Beck and Fernandez decided to stay at her place. On February 28, 1949, Delphine became excited. Fernandez and Beck wanted to calm her and gave her sleeping pills. Downing's daughter saw everything and began to cry, which made Beck angry. She tried to choke the child but didn't succeed. Fernandez shot Delphine who was unconscious. Beck drowned Downing's daughter in a basin of water. The couple buried the bodies in the basement. When the neighbors didn't see the Downings, they reported their disappearance.

ARREST AND TRIAL

Having received the call from neighbors on March 1, 1949, the police arrived at the Downing's door and arrested Beck and Fernandez.

Fernandez confessed, saying he was protecting Beck.

Their trial was sensational. The judge convicted Fernandez and Beck of Janet Fay's murder and sentenced them to death.

OUTCOME

On March 8, 1951, Joseph Francel executed both in the electric chair.

ELVIRA AND KATE BENDER

- ◊ **Date of birth:**
- ◊ **Nicknames:** Bloody Benders
- ◊ **Motive:** The sheer thrill
- ◊ **Number of victims:** 11
- ◊ **Date of murders:** 1869 - 1872
- ◊ **Date of arrest:** Unknown
- ◊ **Murder method:** Hitting with a hammer - Cutting their throats
- ◊ **Known victims:** Travelers
- ◊ **Crime location:** Labette County, Kansas, United States
- ◊ **Status:** Some stated that a small band of riders caught up with the bloodthirsty family and killed them. Others thought that the Benders escaped out on the trackless prairie or had slipped aboard a train in Thayer.

BACKGROUND

When the American Civil War was over, the United States government moved the Osage Indians from Kansas to a new Indian Territory in Oklahoma. Homesteaders occupied the new land. In October 1870, some families of spiritualists settled in and around the township of Osage in western Labette County. One of them was the Benders family. John Bender, Sr. and John Bender, Jr. registered 160 acres of land located near the Great Osage Trail. It was the only open road for traveling further west. Elvira Bender and daughter Kate joined male Benders in the fall of 1871 after they had built a cabin, a barn with corral, and a well. The Benders decided to divide the cabin into two rooms by a canvas wagon-cover. They used the smaller room at the back as a living area, while the front lodging was converted into a store where they sold a few dry goods. The front section also contained the kitchen with a dining table, where travelers could stop for a meal or even for the night. Kate and Elvira Bender also planted a 2-acre vegetable garden and apple orchard north of the cabin.

Sixty-year-old John Bender, Sr. spoke little English. The Emporia News edition of May 23, 1873 identified him with the name of William Bender. 55-year-old Elvira Bender, who also spoke very little English, was so unfriendly that her neighbors called her a "she-devil." Twenty-five-year-old John Bender, Jr. was handsome with brown hair and a mustache. He spoke English fluently but with a German accent. Kate Bender was around 23 and attractive. She spoke English well with a little accent. A self-proclaimed healer and psychic, Kate distributed flyers which told about her supernatural powers and ability to cure illnesses. She conducted séances and gave lectures on spiritualism, for which she gained popularity for advocating free love. Kate's notoriety was a great attraction for the Benders' inn. Kate and John, Jr. regularly attended Sunday school in nearby Harmony Grove.

According to the newspapers, Elvira was born Almira Hill Mark in the Adirondack Mountains. She married Simon Mark. The couple had 12 children. Later, she married William Stephen Griffith. Some suspected Elvira of murdering several husbands, but none of these rumors were ever proven. Others believed Kate was Elvira's fifth daughter, born Sarah Eliza Mark. A Bible recovered from the Bender home had an inscription that John Jr. was born John Gebhardt. However, no other proof of his identity exists. Some of the family neighbors claimed that John and Kate were not brother and sister, but husband and wife.

COLLAPSE

George Newton Longcor and Mary Ann, his infant daughter, left Kansas, to resettle in Iowa in the winter of 1872. Nobody saw them again. In the spring of 1873, Dr. William Henry York, Longcor's neighbor, went looking for them and questioned homesteaders along the trail. On March 9, Dr. York began the return journey from Fort Scott to Independence but never arrived home. He had two brothers: Colonel Ed York and Alexander M. York. Both knew of their brother's travel plans and, when he did not return home, they began an all-out search for the missing man. Colonel York, having a company of fifty men, questioned every traveler along the trail and visited all the homesteads.

Colonel York visited the Benders' inn with Mr. Johnson on March 28, 1873. He told them that his brother had gone missing and asked if they had seen him. The Benders acknowledged Dr. York had stayed with them and suggested the possibility that he had troubles with Indians. Dr. York's brother did not deny such a possibility and remained for dinner. Some days later, Elvira Bender threatened a woman with knives. On April 3, after being informed about that, Colonel York returned to the inn with armed men. York repeated the claim several times, and Elvira became furious. She declared the woman was a witch who had cursed her coffee and ordered the men to leave her house. Kate asked York to return alone the following Friday night. She wanted to use her "clairvoyant" abilities to help him find his brother. The men with York believed the Benders were guilty and wanted to hang them all, but York insisted that they had to find evidence.

At the same time, neighboring communities began to make allegations that the Osage community was responsible for the disappearances.

They organized a meeting in the Harmony Grove schoolhouse. Seventy-five locals, including both John Bender, Sr. and John Bender, Jr. and Colonel York attended the meeting. All present agreed that a search warrant would be obtained to search every homestead between Big Hill Creek and Drum Creek. Nobody noticed for several days that the Benders had fled.

Billy Tole was driving cattle past the Bender's house three days after the meeting. He noticed that the farm animals were unfed, and the inn was left. The weather was inclement, and several days passed before the township trustee could investigate the abandonment. The trustee asked volunteers for help, and several hundred came to form a search party with Colonel York. When the party arrived, they found the inn empty of food, clothing, and personal belongings. The searchers noticed an unpleasant odor which traced to a trap nailed shut door underneath a bed. They opened the pitfall and found clotted blood on the floor of the empty room square at the bottom.

The volunteers broke the stone slab floor with sledgehammers, but they did not find any bodies there. They determined that the smell was from the blood that had soaked into the soil. The men then probed the ground around the cabin using metal rods, especially in the disturbed soil of the vegetable garden and orchard. Dr. York's body was found there later that evening, buried face down. After midnight, the men retired for the night. The following morning, they dug another nine suspected grave sites and found another eight bodies in seven of the nine suspected graves. They

also found one victim in the well, along with several body parts. The newspapers reported that all, but one had had their heads bashed with a hammer and their throats cut. The men found the body of a young girl with no injuries, and it was supposed that she had been buried alive. After seeing the mutilated victims, the crowd was so furious that a man named Brockman, a friend of the Benders, was hung from a beam in the inn until unconscious, revived and questioned about what he knew, then hanged again. After the third hanging, the angry mass of people released him.

Souvenir hunters destroyed the cabin and took everything, including the bricks and the stones lining the well.

State Senator Alexander York promised to pay a $1,000 reward for the Bender family's arrest. Kansas Governor Thomas A. Osborn proposed a $2,000 reward for the apprehension of all four.

It is supposed that when a guest stayed at the Benders' inn, the owners gave the guest a seat at the table situated over a trap door leading into the cellar. The victim was sitting with the back to the curtain, and Kate entertained the guest, while John Bender, Sr. or John Bender, Jr. came from behind the curtain and struck the victim with a hammer. One of the women cut the victim's throat to ensure death. They then dropped the body through the trap door. The Benders stripped the body in the cellar and later buried it somewhere on the property, often in the orchard.

Two men who had come to the inn to experience Kate's psychic powers stayed on for dinner. They had refused to sit at the table next to the cloth and preferred to eat their meal at the shop counter. Kate became rude toward them, and a bit later, the two Bender men appeared from behind the curtain. The customers began to feel discomfort and decided to leave, a move that saved their lives.

The searchers found more than a dozen bullet holes in the roof and sides of the cabin. The reporters later speculated that some of the victims had attempted to fight back after being hit with the hammer.

Detectives discovered the Benders' wagon, abandoned with a starving team of horses just outside the city limits of Thayer. It was confirmed that the family had bought train tickets for Humboldt. John Jr. and Kate left the train at Chanute and caught the train to the terminus in Red River County near Denison, Texas. They traveled to an outlaw colony which was situated between Texas and New Mexico. The lawmen did not pursue them being afraid they would never return. Elvira and John Bender, Sr. did not leave the train at Humboldt but instead continued north to Kansas City, where they purchased tickets for St. Louis, Missouri.

Several groups of vigilantes searched for the Benders. Many stories say that one vigilante group caught the Benders. The vigilantes shot all of them but Kate, whom they burned alive. Another group declared they had found the Benders and lynched them before throwing their bodies into the river. No one, however, ever claimed the $3,000 reward.

The search for the Benders continued on and off for the next fifty years.

On October 31, 1889, Mrs. Almira Monroe and Mrs. Sarah Eliza Davis had been arrested in Niles, Michigan several weeks earlier for theft. Officials released them after they had found them not guilty.

According to the Pittsburgh Dispatch, they were then immediately re-arrested for the Bender murders. Mrs. Frances E. McCann, the daughter of one of the Benders' victims, had informed the authorities about the pair in early October after tracking them down. Two Osage township witnesses later confirmed the women's identities. On October 30, Deputy Sheriff LeRoy Dick, the Osage Township trustee arrived in Michigan and arrested the couple.

Mrs. Davis stated that Mrs. Monroe was Ma Bender. She later signed an affidavit, while Monroe continued to reject the identification and in turn accused Sarah Eliza of being Kate Bender. Sheriff Dick escorted the two to Oswego, Kansas. Seven members of a thirteen-member panel affirmed the identification and sent them for trial.

Judge Calvin found that the affidavits were enough proof that the women could never be convicted. He discharged them both. Further examination is impossible because the affidavits and other papers are missing from the file in LaBette County. While the two women were liars and criminals, as their defense attorney acknowledged, many people doubted their identification as the Benders and the charges were weak.

Colonel York found a knife with a four inch tapered blade hidden in a mantel clock in the Bender house. In 1923, York's wife donated it to the Kansas Museum of History, but it is not on display. The knife, still bearing reddish-brown stains on the blade, can be seen upon request.

MEDIA

Episode 4, titled "Kate Bender," of the 1954 television series Stories of the Century, focused on only the son and daughter.

Manly Wade Wellman's 1960 Candle of the Wicked tells the events leading up to the discovery of the Bender killings.

The 1967 Big Valley, Season 3, Episode 6, "Ladykiller" depicts the story of the Bloody Benders.

Ken Hodgson's 1999 novel The Hell Benders focuses on the search for the Benders after the discovery of their crimes.

In 2004, Scott Phillips wrote a novel Cottonwood, which features Kate Bender in a supporting role; the second half of the book takes place during the trial of two alleged surviving members of the Bender Family.

2006 Season 1, episode 15 of the TV series Supernatural, titled "The Benders," alludes to the historical Benders in several ways.

In Lyle Brandt's 2009 novel Massacre Trail the Benders are responsible for several homestead killings and are brought down by Marshal Jack Slade.

Episode 8 of The Librarians, titled "And the Heart of Darkness," portrays the Benders as serial murderers who escaped justice.

Travel Channel's show Mysteries at the Museum features the story of the Benders in the "Hitchcock's Birds, Hope Diamond, Phineas Gang" episode.

Harold Schechter, in his Bloodlands short story collection, covered the Bender family in "Little Slaughterhouse on the Prairie."

DEBRA BROWN

- ◊ **Date of birth:** November 11, 1962
- ◊ **Motive:** Racial
- ◊ **Number of victims:** 8
- ◊ **Date of murders:** May – July 1984
- ◊ **Date of arrest:** July 20, 1984
- ◊ **Murder method:** Strangulation
- ◊ **Known victims:** Vernita Wheat, 9; Tamika Turks, 7; Donna Williams, 25; Virginia Temple and her daughter Rachelle, 9; Tonnie Storey, 15; Marlene Walters, 44; a 77-year-old man
- ◊ **Crime location:** Indiana, Ohio, Illinois, United States
- ◊ **Status:** On June 23, 1986, sentenced to death in Indiana

BACKGROUND

Debra Brown suffered head trauma as a child, and a psychiatrist diagnosed her with a dependent personality disorder. She was one of 11 children and borderline intellectually disabled.

In 1983, Brown was engaged to another man when she met Coleman. She left her family and moved in with him shortly afterward. Debra had no history of violence, or any record of trouble with the law until she met Coleman.

MURDERS

In May 1984, Coleman and Brown committed their first crime when they killed nine-year-old Vernita Wheat from Wisconsin. Alton Coleman met her mother, Juanita Wheat, and on May 29, 1984, Coleman stole Vernita and took her to Waukegan. On June 19, 1984, the police officers discovered Vernita's badly decomposed corpse in an abandoned building nearby Coleman's grandmother's apartment. The experts determined Vernita had been raped, and the cause of death was ligature strangulation.

In June 1984, nine-year-old Annie and her niece, seven-year-old Tamika Turks were walking back from the candy store to their home when Brenda Brown and Alton Coleman confronted them.

Brown and Coleman persuaded them to go into the woods to play around.

Once there, they tore Tamika's shirt into small strips which they used to bind and gag the children. Tamika started to cry; Brown held her nose and mouth while Coleman came on her chest.

Brown and Coleman carried Tamika a short distance away and forced Annie to perform oral sex on them both, then Coleman raped her. They then choked her until she lost consciousness. When she awoke, they were gone.

Brown and Coleman strangled Tamika with a flexible strip of the bedsheet. She was found dead in the bushes nearby. The policemen later found the same fabric in the apartment shared by two criminals. Annie received injuries so deep that her entrails were protruding into her vagina.

Coleman befriended Virginia Temple in Toledo, Ohio where they had arrived on July 5. She was the mother of several children. Virginia had stopped communicating with her relatives concerning the welfare of her children. Coleman and Brown entered Temple's home and strangled Virginia and her eldest child, 9-year-old Rachelle, to death. The officials discovered their bodies in a crawl space. The same morning, Coleman and Brown entered Frank and Dorothy Duvendack' home in Toledo. Coleman bound the pair with appliance and phone cords, taking the money and their car. Later that day, Coleman and Brown visited the home of Reverend Millard Gay and his wife, Kathryn in Dayton, Ohio. The two stayed with the Gays, and on July 10, the Gays dropped off Coleman and Brown in downtown Cincinnati, Ohio.

On July 12, a 15-year-old girl Tonnie Storey disappeared in the Over-the-Rhine neighborhood of Cincinnati. Eight days later, the officials discovered her raped and murdered body. Under the body, the police officers found a bracelet that had been stolen from the Temples in Toledo.

On July 13, Coleman and Brown bicycled into Norwood. Coleman and Brown inquired about a camper Harry Walters and his 45-year-old wife, Marlene, had offered for sale. While Walters and Coleman discussed the deal with Coleman, Coleman picked up a wooden candlestick and hit Walters with it on the back of the head. Harry Walters survived, but his wife had been raped and beaten to death. Sheri Walters, the couple's daughter, returned home from work and found her father still alive, but unconscious and her mother dead at the bottom of the basement steps. The coroner indicated Marlene Walters had been cudgeled on the head approximately 20 to 25 times. The Walters' car was missing, as well as jewelry, shoes, and money which had been stolen.

Two days later, Walters's car was found left in Kentucky, where the criminals had abducted Oline Carmical, Jr., a college professor from Williamsburg. The couple drove back to Dayton with Carmical locked in the boot of his car. On July 17, Coleman and Brown abandoned a stolen vehicle in Dayton, Ohio. The authorities rescued Carmical, who was still locked in the trunk.

The criminals returned to Reverend and Mrs. Gay' home in Dayton. Mr. Gay recognized Coleman, who was the subject of a vast nationwide search, and Coleman accosted the Gays with guns. Coleman and Brown did not kill Millard and Kathryn but took their car and drove back toward Evanston, Illinois. On the way, they killed 75-year-old Eugene Scott in Indianapolis and stole his car.

ARREST AND TRIAL

On July 20, the authorities arrested Coleman and Brown in Evanston, Illinois. As Coleman and Brown walked across a crossroad, they passed in front of a man in a car who was from Coleman's neighborhood in Waukegan. The man recognized Coleman and drove to a gas station to notify the police. Two sergeants, patrolling the park, saw Coleman and Brown going in different directions. Coleman had no identification and denied he was Alton Coleman. At the same time, two other officers stopped Brown, searched her, and found a gun in her bag. The police officers took the pair into custody and transported to the Evanston Police Department, where experts identified both by their fingerprints.

At the police station, officers strip-searched Coleman and found a steak knife between two pairs of sweat socks he was wearing. A week after the arrest, more than 50 law enforcement officials from different states, where the two had committed crimes, met to plan their strategy for prosecuting Coleman and Brown. Ohio was decided to be given the first attempt at sentencing.

The state of Ohio found Coleman and Brown guilty of the rape and murder of Marlene Walters in Norwood and Tonnie Storey in Cincinnati. The criminals were both sentenced to death, and the appeals process began. Between 1985 and 2002, Coleman's case was sent to the U.S. Supreme Court several times, but his multiple arguments that his conviction and death sentence were unconstitutional failed to sway the justices.

Alton Coleman was executed in the death chamber at the Southern Ohio Correctional Facility in Lucasville, Ohio by lethal injection on April 26, 2002.

Ohio sentenced Coleman to two death sentences. States Illinois and Indiana sentenced him to one death sentence. He was the only person in the United States to have death sentences in three states at the time of his execution.

Brown was sentenced to be executed in Ohio for her complicity in the crimes. In 1991, Governor Richard Celeste commuted her death sentence to life in prison for her low IQ scores. Celeste was a staunch opponent of capital punishment. A week after commuting, he left the office. The authorities also gave her a death sentence for the murder of Tamika Turks. However, in 2018, that sentence was commuted to 140 years imprisonment.

OUTCOME

Brown is currently serving her sentence without the possibility of parole at the Dayton Correctional Institution in Dayton, Ohio.

Brown finally apologized to the families of her and Coleman's victims in a video in 2005.

JUDY BUENOANO

- ◊ **Date of birth:** April 4, 1943
- ◊ **Nickname:** Florida's Black Widow
- ◊ **Motive:** Life insurance money
- ◊ **Number of victims:** Up to four
- ◊ **Date of murders:** 1971 – 1980
- ◊ **Date of arrest:** March 31, 1984
- ◊ **Murder method:** Poisoning
- ◊ **Known victims:** Her husband James Goodyear, her boyfriends: Bobby Joe Morris and Gerald Dossett; her son: Michael Buenoano
- ◊ **Crime location:** Colorado, Florida
- ◊ **Status:** Death by electric chair, 1998

BACKGROUND

Judy had a difficult childhood as many other criminals claim. She was born Judias Welty, on April 4, 1943, in Quanah, Texas, the daughter of a farm laborer. She was of Latina ethnic background. Welty and her mother were not close. When Judy was only four, her mum died of tuberculosis. This caused the separation of the family. Judy's grandparents took her with her infant brother Robert to live with them, while two older children were adopted.

Her father moved to Roswell, New Mexico, remarried and took Judy and Robert to live with his new wife. Judy's father and stepmother abused her. She was miserable there. She supposedly was beaten, starved, forced to work long hours as a virtual slave, hardly an ideal upbringing for a teenage girl. At the age of 14, she attempted to attack her parents and two stepbrothers. The authorities sentenced Judy to 2 months in prison. Having been released, she didn't come back to her abusive family but went to a reform school. In 1959, at sixteen, Judy graduated from the Foothills High School in Albuquerque.

She got her first job in 1960 working as a nursing assistant in Roswell. Anna Schultz was her assumed name. She gave birth to an extramarital son in 1961, and Judy christened him Michael Schultz.

MURDERS

On January 21, 1962, Judy married for the first time. Her husband was James Goodyear, and he was an air force officer. On January 16, 1966, Judy gave birth to their first child, James, Jr. James Goodyear adopted her illegitimate son

Michael. In 1967 the family moved to Orlando, Florida where they had a daughter, Kimberley.

In 1968 Judy opened her first business, the Conway Acres Child Care Center using funds from her husband. Having done a tour of duty in Vietnam, James Goodyear, Sr. returned home. Only three months later, doctors put him to the U.S. Naval Hospital in Orlando suffering from mysterious symptoms. On September 15th, 1971, he died. Judy got cash for his three life insurance policies. At the end of that year, her house was in a fire, so, Judy received $90,000 from the insurers.

Soon she met a new boyfriend Bobby Joe Morris who lived in Pensacola. In 1972 Judy moved there to live with him. Her son Michael darkened her new life because he was mentally challenged. She placed him with a residential foster family.

In 1977 Bobby Morris moved to Trinidad, Colorado and a little later Judy and her family (including Michael) joined him there. Before leaving Pensacola, she again suffered from another house fire and got another insurance payout.

On January 4, 1978, soon after she moved to Colorado, Bobby Joe became ill and was admitted to the hospital. His doctors didn't know the cause and discharged him.

On January 21 of that year, he was taken back to the hospital where he died, and again Judy capitalized the insurance policies.

Bobby's family suspected that he had been murdered. Judy and Bobbi visited his hometown in Alabama in 1974. In a motel room, the police found a dead man from Florida. Someone had shot the man in the chest and cut his throat. On his deathbed, Bobbi Joe admitted he had taken part in that murder.

In 1978 Judy legally changed her and her children's surname to Buenoano, which means Goodyear in Spanish.

The family returned to Pensacola. Her son, Michael Buenoano, had done poorly in school and in 1979 he joined the army. He was based in Georgia. Soon he became seriously ill, and doctors diagnosed him as suffering from arsenic poisoning. His upper and lower limbs were weak, and doctors from the military hospital gave him metal leg braces, and he was sent home. His mother took care of him because he couldn't use his hands and was unable to walk.

In the Spring, 1980, Judy decided to go canoeing on the East River. She took Michael and his younger brother James. Sadly, the canoe overturned. Judy and James were able to get out of the water, but Michael, weighed down by the heavy braces, drowned.

Again, Judy received Michael's military life insurance, which was $20,000.

Judy opened a beauty salon and began dating a businessman named John Gentry II from Pensacola. She convinced him to take out a life insurance policy in 1982 and later increased the size to $500,000. Judy also insisted he take vitamins, which made him feel dizzy. She told him to double the dose when he felt worse.

In 1983 Judy declared she was pregnant and John was going to celebrate that. There was a loud explosion when he started his car. John got serious injuries but survived. After a few days, he could answer the police's questions. He suspected Judy.

The police learned that Judy was not pregnant and had no medical qualifications. She had been telling her friends that John had a fatal illness.

Some of the suspected vitamin capsules were found to contain arsenic; however, the police didn't see enough evidence to incriminate Judy for attempted murder.

ARREST AND TRIAL

Further search of Judy's bedroom led the officers to discover tape and wire, which matched the remains from the bomb in Gentry's car. Later the police also traced the dynamite and linked Judy through telephone records. She was duly arrested and bailed on the charge of attempted murder of John Gentry.On January 11, 1984, the police arrested her again and charged her with first-degree murder of her son, Michael. In February the authorities exhumed the body of Bobby Joe Morris and found arsenic. The same year the body of James Goodyear was exhumed in March and arsenic was found.

Judy was sued separately for each murder, including the attempted one. On June 6th, 1984, for the killing of her son, she was sentenced to life imprisonment without parole for the first twenty-five years.

OUTCOME

Judy Buenoano was the first woman executed in Florida since 1848. On March 30, 1998, she was executed in the electric chair and wished her grandson to never know his granny was a murderer.

CAROL MARY BUNDY

- ◊ **Date of birth:** August 26, 1942
- ◊ **Nicknames:** The Hollywood Slasher, The Sunset Strip Killer, The Sunset Strip Slayer
- ◊ **Motive:** Sexual adventures
- ◊ **Number of victims:** Up to 2
- ◊ **Date of murders:** July–August 1980
- ◊ **Date of arrest:** August 11, 1980
- ◊ **Murder method:** Shooting and decapitation – an accomplice of Douglas Clark
- ◊ **Known victims:** Unnamed prostitute and a part-time country singer Jack Murray aged 45
- ◊ **Crime location:** Los Angeles, California, USA
- ◊ **Status:** Sentenced to prison terms of twenty-five years-to-life on the count of participating in the murder of one of Clark's victims and twenty-seven years-to-life for the killing of Jack Murray and the use of a gun on May 31, 1983. Died in prison on December 9, 2003.

BACKGROUND

Carol Mary Bundy didn't have a happy childhood. Her parents were alcoholics. Carol's mother died young, and her father sexually abused her when she was only 11.

Bundy's father remarried and put her in different foster homes. She married an older man who was 56 while she was 17.

At the age of 37, Bundy met Doug Clark. She had just divorced her third husband, who was an abusive person. They had two sons. She had an affair with her apartment block manager, part-time country singer Jack Murray. Carol tried to suborn Murray's wife, hoping she would leave him. Murray's wife forced him to expel Bundy from the block. Carol continued to appear consistently at places where he was singing.

She first met Clark in 1980 at a bar called Little Nashville, where he was performing. Doug Clark soon moved in with Bundy, and they learned that they shared dark sexual fantasies.

MURDERS

Clark brought prostitutes back to their apartment to have threesomes. When

Doug took an interest in an 11-year-old neighbor, he asked Bundy to help him entrap the girl and make her pose for pornographic shots. Clark quickly outgrew pedophilia and started to talk about how much he would like to kill a girl during sex. He convinced Bundy to buy two automatic guns for him. Doug Clark reportedly wanted to fulfill his fantasy of killing a woman during sex and feeling her vaginal contractions during the death spasms.

One night, in June 1980, Clark came home and told Bundy about two teenagers, Gina Narano and Cynthia Chandler. He had picked them up on the Sunset Strip and murdered the two young girls. Clark had ordered them to perform fellatio on him. He shot them both in the head before taking them to a garage and raping their dead bodies. He had then thrown the bodies near the Ventura Freeway, and the next day the police found them. Carol M. Bundy phoned the police, confessing to having some knowledge of the crimes, but refused to give any clues as to Clark's identity. Clark assured Bundy that, if the authorities arrested either of them, he would take the blame.

Clark murdered two prostitutes, Karen Jones and Exxie Wilson only twelve days after the previous murders. He lured them into his car, shot them, removed Wilson's head, and dumped the bodies in sight. Clark brought the head back to their apartment and put it in the refrigerator. Bundy put make-up on it before Clark used it for another "attack of necrophilia." Some days later, the couple put the freshly cleaned head in a box and threw it in an alleyway.

Meantime, Carol Bundy continued to attend Murray's performances. One day she spoke with him there, and after a few drinks, Bundy told Murray about the crimes she and Clark had committed. Murray was shocked and mentioned that he could tell the police. After a show, in August 1980, to prevent this, Bundy entrapped Murray in his van to have sex. She shot and decapitated him inside the truck. Bundy, however, left various clues in the van, including shell casings. Two days later, Bundy's co-workers called the police after she confessed she had murdered Murray. When the police came, she gave a full confession to crimes she and Clark had committed.

ARREST AND TRIAL

After Clark's arrest, the police found the murder weapons at his workplace. At his trial, he blamed Bundy for everything. Bundy accepted a plea bargain and was sentenced to fifty-two-years-to-life imprisonment.

OUTCOME

At the age of 61, Carol Bundy died in prison from heart failure on December 9, 2003.

PATTY CANNON

- ◊ **Date of birth:** c. 1760 or 1759 or 1769
- ◊ **Other names:** Lucretia P. Cannon, Patricia Cannon, Lucretia Hanly, Martha Cannon
- ◊ **Motive:** Kidnapping for sale, slave stealing, and illegal trading
- ◊ **Number of victims:** 4 up to 11 and more
- ◊ **Date of murders:** 1820 – 1829
- ◊ **Date of arrest:** 1829
- ◊ **Murder method:** beating, shooting
- ◊ **Victims:** men, women, children
- ◊ **Crime location:** Maryland, Delaware, Delmarva Peninsula, Chesapeake Bay, Philadelphia, Pennsylvania, New Jersey, Georgia, Southern United States
- ◊ **Status:** Suicide in County jail, Georgetown, Sussex County, Delaware

BACKGROUND

Local farmer Jesse Cannon married Patty Cannon and they lived near the town of Reliance, Maryland. He died in 1826.

The couple had at least one daughter, who twice married men engaged in the criminal slave–stealing trade. Their daughter's name is unknown, but Henry Brereton was her first husband. Henry kidnapped black people for sale. In 1811 he went to prison for kidnapping, but he escaped from the Georgetown, Delaware jail. The authorities captured him, convicted him of murder, and he was hanged.

Cannon's daughter married Joe Johnson who became her most notorious associate in crimes.

The gang consisted of white criminals and black men used as decoys.

In 1808 the U.S. Congress forbade the importation of slaves. At that time, because of the ban, the cash value of slaves increased, bringing over $1,000 in the South, creating a significant stimulus for kidnappers. Many free Black Americans lived in Cannon's neighborhood in Maryland and Delaware and were easy targets for her kidnapping raids. It was riskier to kidnap enslaved Black Americans, as their white owners would protest. The murder of white slave traders was similarly a severe crime.

The gang hid chained captives in the basement and the attic. They took slaves in covered wagons to Cannon's

Ferry where they would meet a tugboat sailing down the Nanticoke River to slave markets in Georgia.

The gang continued its activities for many years. Local authorities unwillingly halted the illegal transactions as they might be afraid of the gang's violent reputation. When Patty Cannon learned the police were approaching, she would escape across the state border and away from the police.

Victims testified that Joe Johnson used leg irons to keep the captives. He severely whipped prisoners who insisted on freedom. Johnson's wife, Patty's daughter, stated that she liked watching him beating the victims.

Lydia Smith, a free black woman, aged 25, witnessed a beating before moving to Johnson's Tavern; the gang kept her in Cannon's home for five months until she was shipped south with a lot of people being sold into slavery.

MURDERS, ARREST, AND TRIAL

In May 1822 the gang was convicted. The police sentenced Joe Johnson to the pillory and 39 lashes, and the authorities carried out the sentence. Cannon and several gang members, though accused with Johnson, did not go to trial nor receive a punishment.

A tenant farmer was doing plowing and discovered bodies at Cannon's farm in Delaware in 1829, and so the local authorities indicted her in April 1829 for the following: (1) an infant female on April 26, 1822; (2) a male child on April 26, 1822; (3) an adult male on October 1, 1820; and (4) a "Negro boy" on June 1, 1824.

James Rogers, the Attorney General of Delaware, signed the four indictments. Witness Cyrus James confirmed he saw Cannon carry an injured "black child not yet dead out in her apron, but that it never returned." Cannon purchased Cyrus when he was seven; he had grown up in her household and participated in the crimes.

OUTCOME

On May 11, 1829, Cannon died in her cell in her late sixties. Sources differ on whether she died of natural causes or committed suicide (poisoning).

The jailers buried her in the prison's graveyard. In the 20th century, that land became a parking lot, and her skeleton was unearthed. They reburied it near the new jail but separated her skull from the rest of the remains to show it in different venues. In 1961 her skull was loaned to the Dover Public Library.

SUZAN BEAR CARSON

- ◇ **Date of birth:** September 14, 1941
- ◇ **Nickname:** Witch-Killer
- ◇ **Motive:** Drugs and mysticism
- ◇ **Number of victims:** 30-year-old Jon Charles Hellyar, 22-year-old Keryn Barnes, Clark Stephens
- ◇ **Date of murders:** 1981-1983
- ◇ **Date of arrest:** 1983
- ◇ **Murder method:** stabbing, shooting
- ◇ **Known victims:** 3+
- ◇ **Crime location:** Northern California and the San Francisco Bay Area
- ◇ **Status:** Sentenced to 75-years-to-life imprisonment

BACKGROUND

In 1977, Susan Barnes began a relationship with James Carson. They married and became involved in illicit drugs and mysticism. At some moment, Carson wrote a letter to his daughter telling her that God had given him the name Michael and he became Michael Bear, so Susan took the name Suzan Bear. They also declared their belonging to the Muslim faith.

In 1980, the Carsons decided to return to the United States after a year-long trip to Europe. They moved to San Francisco, California and remained involved with the counterculture and drugs.

The Carsons committed crimes based on a shared missionary philosophy bent on exterminating individuals they considered to be "witches." The pair kept a list of targeted individuals including celebrities and political figures such as Johnny Carson and President Ronald Reagan.

The Carsons were 30-year-old hippies from San Francisco, who managed a large pot farm in Humboldt County, California.

MURDERS

In San Francisco, the couple shared an apartment with an aspiring actress Keryn Barnes, who was 22. In March 1981, she was found dead. The killer had stabbed her thirteen times and crushed her skull before wrapping it in a blanket and hiding it in the basement. The prime suspects were the Carsons. They, however, disappeared before police found the body. The family later confessed to killing Keryn after Suzan had decided Keryn was a witch.

The pair escaped to a mountain hiding place near Grants Pass, Oregon, where they stayed until Spring 1982. They moved to Alderpoint, California where they lived and worked on a farm where marijuana was grown. According to other farm workers, the Carsons were anarchists who stood for revolution.

In May 1982, Michael had a dispute with Clark Stephens, who was a worker on the farm. Carson shot Stephens, burned the body and buried it in the woods.

The Carsons fled, but the Humboldt County sheriff considered them to be suspects. Upon searching the belongings they left behind, detectives found a manifesto they had written which called for the assassination of then President Ronald Reagan; however, the police had difficulties tracking down the Carsons over the coming years.

In January 1983, the Carsons were hitchhiking near Bakersfield and 30-year-old Jon Charles Hellyar, who was driving to Santa Rosa, gave them a ride.

Suzan decided that Hellyar was a witch, so, they had to kill him. While Hellyar was driving on Route 101 in Sonoma County, an argument and then a physical fight broke out between him and the Carsons. Hellyar had to stop the vehicle. The conflict intensified outside the car, and Suzan stabbed Hellyar while he and Michael struggled over a gun. Michael got control of the weapon and killed Hellyar in view of passing drivers, one of whom called the police. A high-speed chase ensued as the couple attempted to escape in Hellyar's car, but they were arrested.

ARREST AND TRIAL

The Carsons called a press conference to confess to the murders of Hellyar, Stephens, and Keryn Barnes. Before trial, they denied their confessions and entered pleas of not guilty. In June 1984, the authorities convicted the Carsons of Barnes' murder and sentenced them to 25 years in prison. Later, they were convicted of murdering Stephens and Hellyar. The couple received sentences of 50 years to life and 75 years to life. Michael serves his sentence at Mule Creek State Prison and Suzan at Central California Women's Facility.

OUTCOME

They declared that they killed Barnes because they believed she had made a false conversion to their religion. Their justification for the second killing was that Stephens had sexually abused Suzan. They also stated that Hellyar had called Suzan a "witch" and sexually assaulted her. From their conviction and through their incarceration, they showed no remorse for their crimes.

MARY CLEMENT

- ◊ **Date of birth:** February 16, 1863
- ◊ **Other names:** Mary Kleman, Mary Klemann, Mary Clayman, Mary Klaman, Mary Clemens
- ◊ **Number of victims:** 4
- ◊ **Date of murders:** 1880 - 1885
- ◊ **Date of arrest:** June 1884
- ◊ **Murder method:** Poisoning
- ◊ **Known victims:** Her parents and two of her sisters
- ◊ **Crime location**: Iowa, United States
- ◊ **Status:** Sentenced to a year in jail. Died at the age of 81.

BACKGROUND

Mary Clement was born in the little village of Harlange. Her parents were Michel and Margarite Clement. Mary was the second of the couple's five daughters. In 1871, the family immigrated to the United States, settling in Dubuque, where three years later, the last daughter, Annie, would be born. Mary was described as a slender and rather pretty girl. She was prepossessing in manner, but due to a defect in her spinal column, she had only partial control over her legs and feet.

MURDERS

In 1880, Mary's six-year-old sister Annie was suddenly seized with convulsions and died shortly after on August 1, 1880. Her death was later attributed to overeating before going to bed. During the following years, her 54-year-old mother died on July 24, 1884, her 49-year-old father on March 28, 1885, and her 13-year-old sister Lena on August 9, 1884. They all died in similar circumstances and passed away from convulsions or heart failure after suffering through an unidentifiable illness.

ARREST AND TRIAL

Mary moved in with her sister Catherine, her husband, Michael Freres and their two children in Rose Hill two months following the burial of her father. She cooked meals for the family on several occasions, and each time, they would be overtaken by violent vomiting and spasms. Michael grew suspicious of Mary, as she always refused to eat any of the soup she served. One day, Michael found a pack of grayish-colored powder in the backyard. In the afternoon, after eating some soup, he again began vomiting. While eating, Michael noticed sediment in his plate that looked like the strange powder. Upon further examination, he found more of the substance in his wife and the children's plates. Puzzled, Michael brought the powder and the plates for analysis in Evanston. The attending physicians, Dr. Isaac Poole and Professor H. S. Corbart, revealed that the powder contained arsenic. Shortly after this discovery, the officials arrested Mary Clement.

While imprisoned, Mary initially furiously protested that she was innocent, crying for two days. She claimed that her sister had accused her of the single reason of obtaining $100, which Clement had. However, when a reporter later questioned Clement, she confessed not only to poisoning her sister's family, but also killing her mother, father, and little sister. Mary explained that a feeling to end her ailing mother's misery had overtaken her. When asked if money was her motive, Mary claimed that she "hated the money." After questioning the same day, she experienced a hysterical fit, threw herself at her cot and demanded to see a priest.

Two days after, Dr. Bluthardt interviewed her, and during the questioning, Mary stated to have never made her confession or that if she did, she remembered nothing of it. Bluthardt denied Clement's insanity when later asked if he thought that she was. He believed she suffered from several disorders that made her extremely nervous and sensitive.

At the trial, Mary observed the procedure closely, but did it so abnormally calmly and expressed nervousness so seldom, that even the press noticed how out of her character it was. Michael Freres was the main witness who presented that there was evidence of arsenic poisoning, and the jury quickly sentenced Mary Clement to a year in jail. The following month, Clement wrote a letter confessing to her crimes, including her youngest sister's murder, shocking associates who still considered her innocent. In it, she expressed her pleasure with the short sentence.

OUTCOME

After the release, Clement moved out to Los Angeles. She worked there as a domestic servant for a wealthy family. According to the family members, she never talked about her past, but everybody knew her as a nice old lady who liked to wear fancy hats. Mary Clement died at the age of 81. She was later buried at St. Henry's Church in Chicago, in the Freres family plot.

CYNTHIA COFFMAN

- ◊ **Date of birth:** January 19, 1962
- ◊ **Motive:** Kidnapping, rape, and robberies
- ◊ **Number of victims:** 2
- ◊ **Date of murders:** October–November 1986
- ◊ **Date of arrest:** November 14, 1986
- ◊ **Murder method:** Strangulation
- ◊ **Known victims:** 32-year-old Sandra Neary, 35-year-old Pamela Simmons, 20-year-old Corinna Dell Novis, and 19-year-old Lynel Murray
- ◊ **Crime location:** California, Arizona, USA
- ◊ **Status:** On August 31, 1989, sentenced to death in San Bernardino County, California

BACKGROUND

Cynthia Lynn Coffman was born in St. Louis, Missouri. Her mother raised her alone after their father left the family. Cynthia's mother tried to give her and her brothers away. At the age of 18, Coffman married and became a mother. Her marriage did not last long. She and a friend decided to move to Arizona, where Cynthia met James Marlow who had just gotten out of jail. They married in Tennessee, used methamphetamine, and soon began to commit violent crimes.

MURDERS

The first murder happened in Costa Mesa, California, on October 11, 1986.

Thirty-two-year-old Sandra Neary left her home late in the evening to withdraw money from an ATM. She never returned. The police found her car in a local parking lot. On October 24, hikers found her strangled and decaying body near Corona in Riverside County.

The next victim was Pamela Simmons, age thirty-five. On October 28, magazines and newspapers reported her missing in Bullhead City, Arizona. Somebody found her car near police headquarters. The detectives theorized that the killer had snatched her while she was taking money from the ATM.

On November 7, Corinna Novis, aged 20, disappeared on a similar case in Redlands, California.

On November 12, Cynthia and Marlow kidnapped their fourth victim from an urban shopping mall in broad daylight. Lynel Murray, the 19-year-old psychology student, worked at a dry-cleaning establishment. Her boyfriend found her car outside that shop in Orange County, California.

One more day would pass before the police discovered her naked, strangled body in a Huntington Beach motel room. Along with kidnapping and murder, there was also proof of sexual abuse. The police officers found Corinna Novis's checkbook in a Laguna Niguel trash dumpster, tucked inside a fast-food takeout bag with papers bearing the names of Cynthia Coffman and James Marlow.

ARREST AND TRIAL

Marlow and Coffman were staying at a San Bernardino motel room around the same time, and the manager found stationery bearing the name of Lynel Murray.

On November 14, 1986, the proprietor of a mountain lodge at Big Bear City, California identified his guests as Coffman and Marlow, and he called the police. At 3.00 p.m. a 100-man posse found the suspects hiking along a mountain road in the woods. Coffman and Marlow surrendered without a fight; both wore outfits stolen from the dry-cleaning establishment where Lynel Murray worked.

Within hours, Cynthia led officers to a vineyard near Fontana, where they found Corinna Novis, sodomized and strangled, lying in a shallow grave.

On July 18, 1989, the murder trial finally opened in San Bernardino County. On August 30, the local authorities convicted both defendants across the board, and sentenced both to death. Since California state restored capital punishment under a new statute in 1977, Cynthia Coffman became the first woman sentenced to die.

OUTCOME

A trial in 1992 convicted her of another murder, for which she received a sentence of life imprisonment.

FAYE COPELAND

- ◊ **Date of birth:** August 4, 1921
- ◊ **Motive:** Robberies
- ◊ **Number of victims:** 5-12
- ◊ **Date of murders:** 1986-1989
- ◊ **Date of arrest:** October 17, 1989
- ◊ **Murder method:** Shooting
- ◊ **Known victims:** Dennis K. Murphy, of Normal, Illinois; Wayne Warner, of Bloomington, Illinois; Jimmy Dale Harvey, 27 of Springfield, Missouri; John W. Freeman, 27 of Tulsa, Oklahoma; Paul J. Cowart, 21 of Dardanelle, Arkansas
- ◊ **Crime location:** Mooresville, Missouri, U.S.
- ◊ **Status:** Death, commuted to life imprisonment on August 6, 1999; paroled 2002. In 2003 died of natural causes at a nursing home in her hometown of Chillicothe, Missouri.

BACKGROUND

Faye Copeland was known at birth as Faye Della Wilson. She was born into a dirt-floor home in the crossroads community of Red Star, Arkansas.

Her parents were Rufus and Gladys Wilson. They had no money but raised seven children in the dirt-floor cabin. Faye's education lasted until the eighth grade when she dropped out, so she could earn money for family expenses. At the age of ten, Faye was doing domestic chores like house-cleaning, laundry, and babysitting.

Faye Copeland was seldom known to smile, but she was a hard-working employee.

When Faye met her future husband Ray, she was a fair-haired, pretty, shy girl. After their marriage, Ray was abusive to Faye and their children. It should not be surprising that Faye suffered from Battered Woman Syndrome.

The couple had five children: four boys and a girl, seventeen grandchildren and twenty-five great-grandchildren. The Copeland children left home at the first opportunity because of the unpleasant nature of the family homestead.

Ray and Faye moved their family often and usually without notice or preparation. The Copeland family was frequently impoverished. In the mid-1980s, the family owed $25,000 on farm loans, and they were facing bankruptcy. Perhaps this financial situation caused their serial murder solution.

According to their children's recollections, Faye never dared cross her husband. The Copeland family kept to themselves. They had no close friends and did not attend church.

MURDERS

The crimes of these two great-grandparents are difficult to believe. Serial killers usually start their murder profile at a younger age.

Since Ray was well-known as a swindler, he could not buy and sell livestock on his own. To solve this problem, he began to pick up drifters and employed them as farm laborers on his property in Mooresville, Missouri.

He took his employees to the market, where they used his bad checks and bought the cattle for him. After the deal, Ray sold the cattle quickly, and the farmhands disappeared without a trace. For a while, the fraud worked, but the police caught up with him and sent Ray to jail once again.

Upon his release, he continued his criminal work. In August 1989, Ray's previous employee, Jack McCormick, called the Crime Stoppers hotline to tell them about the Copelands. McCormick insisted that he had seen human bones on Copeland's farm while he was employed there and claimed that Ray had tried to kill him.

Police was distrustful of the claims, but after checking Ray's criminal record, they continued further investigation. In October 1989, dozens of officers and a team of bloodhounds visited the Copeland farm armed with a search warrant. They discovered the bodies of three young men in a nearby barn. As the search continued, the officers found more bodies, all killed with the same weapon, a .22-caliber Marlin rifle that they later found in the Copeland home.

It became clear that Ray killed his employees in the pursuit of money, but Faye's actions were under question.

ARREST AND TRIAL

In November 1990, Faye Copeland went on trial, and her defense introduced her as an obedient wife and mother who had undergone ill-treatment and beatings from the husband. The judge, however, convicted her of four murders and gave her four death sentences.

OUTCOME

In August 2002, Faye had a stroke which left her unable to speak and partially paralyzed. In September 2002, Governor Bob Holden authorized medical parole for her, fulfilling Faye's wish not to die in prison. They sent Faye to a nursing home in her hometown of Chillicothe, Missouri, where she died of natural causes at the age of 82.

MARY FRANCES CREIGHTON

◊ **Date of birth:** July 29, 1899
◊ **Nickname:** Black Eyed Borgia
◊ **Motive:** Short of money
◊ **Number of victims:** 1–3
◊ **Date of murders:** 1923–1935
◊ **Date of arrest:** October 9, 1935
◊ **Murder method:** Poisoning
◊ **Known victims:** Her brother Ray Avery, 18; her mother-in-law Anna Creighton; her lover's wife Ada Applegate, 34
◊ **Crime location:** New Jersey, New York, USA
◊ **Status:** On July 16, 1936, executed by electrocution at Sing Sing prison in New York

BACKGROUND

The media gave her the nickname "Borgia." She married John Creighton, and the couple had a daughter named Ruth. The police arrested Mary and her husband John for the death of her brother, Raymond Avery. They poisoned him using a lethal dose of arsenic. Mary Creighton had been named as a beneficiary in his insurance policy and inherited her brother's trust fund. Their parents died long before the brother's death. The authorities acquitted Mary after a trial in Newark, New Jersey, but within days of the verdict, they arrested her again for the death of her father-in-law. After a hearing, they found her not guilty. After that verdict, they relocated her to Long Island, New York.

MURDERS

The Creightons made friends with a couple named Everett and Ada Applegate in the town of Baldwin, New York. Everett was thirty-seven; Ada was thirty-four. Everything happened in the peak of the Great Depression, and the Creightons moved in with the Applegates to save money. The Applegates had a twelve-year-old daughter named Agnes. By this time, John and Mary's daughter Ruth was fourteen. Everett Applegate started sexually molesting Ruth. His wife joined them. Soon Ruth's mother also joined them. They also molested the Applegate's young daughter Agnes. In September 1936, Ada Applegate complained of a worsening physical condition, and she went to the hospital. The doctors did not find anything wrong and sent her home. She died several days later. The police started an investigation of the death of Ada and performed an autopsy. They found she died from a massive dose of arsenic.

ARREST AND TRIAL

The police arrested Mary Creighton and Everett Applegate, and a trial began. Creighton admitted to the murder, trying to blame Ada's husband, Everett. She claimed he forced her to do it. Mary had gone to the store and bought the rat poison. They both were found guilty of 1st degree murder with a mandatory death sentence. The defenders appealed but to no avail. Over the next few months Mary fell seriously ill, probably due to hysteria; her legs appeared paralyzed, and she lost a lot of weight.

On the day of the execution, she wore soft slippers, pink pajamas, and a black kimono. Prison staff shaved the back of her head. The guards had to bring her into the death chamber at Sing-Sing Prison in a wheelchair.

Mary seemed almost unconscious. She had seen her daughter Ruth the day before, telling her to take care of her father. Mary was thirty-six at the time, a week before her birthday.

OUTCOME

Mary Creighton was strapped into the electric chair and electrocuted. Everett Applegate was next in line for electrocution.

NANNIE DOSS

- ◊ **Date of birth:** November 4, 1905
- ◊ **Nicknames:** The Giggling Grandma, The Jolly Black Widow, The Lonely-Hearts Killer
- ◊ **Motive:** Life insurance money, search for "the real romance of life."
- ◊ **Number of victims:** 11
- ◊ **Date of murders:** 1927–1954
- ◊ **Date of arrest:** October 1954
- ◊ **Murder method:** Poisoning
- ◊ **Known victims:** Four of her husbands, her mother, her sister Dovie, her grandson Robert, her mother-in-law, and Arlie Lanning's mother
- ◊ **Crime location:** Alabama, North Carolina, Kansas, Oklahoma, United States
- ◊ **Status:** The authorities sentenced her to life imprisonment. Nannie died of leukemia.

BACKGROUND

Nannie was born as Nancy Hazle to James and Lou Hazle in Blue Mountain, Alabama. The family had five children, so Nannie had three sisters and one brother.

She had an unhappy childhood and because of an erratic education, she could not read well. Because her father forced her and other children to work on the family farm, they seldom attended school. Nancy's father forbade them to go to dances and other social events because he did not want men to molest them. When Nannie was a child, her hobby was reading her mom's romance magazines. While reading, she dreamed of her romantic future.

When she was seven, the Hazles decided to visit their relatives in southern Alabama. They took a train, but when the train suddenly stopped, Nannie struck her head against a metal bar. She began suffering severe headaches and blackouts. Nancy blamed her mental destabilization on that train accident.

MURDERS

Nannie Doss, a daughter of Dixie, was born in 1905. Before she reached her teens, local men molested her. When she was 16, she married Charles Braggs, and they had four children in quick succession. Charles was mystified when two of them died suddenly, a few months apart, but Nannie could not explain. When Charles left for work, each child had seemed healthy, but they cried and died in convulsions not long after breakfast.

The Braggs got small insurance payments. Charles Braggs became extremely wary of his wife, Nannie. One day, he took their oldest child and left Nanny with their daughter, Florine. Nannie moved to Cedar Town, Georgia where she met and married Frank Harrelson. Florine was two years old when Frank and Nannie left the child alone in their house. Neighbors found Charles Braggs, and he came for the child. Nannie would not see her daughter for nine years.

In 1945 Florine reunited with Nannie and decided to leave her infant son at her mother's home in Jacksonville, Alabama. She took off to visit her father. Three days later, baby Lee died while in his granny's care. Around three months later, Frank Harrelson fell ill and died within a week. Nannie got the insurance money, bought ten acres of land and built a small house outside Jacksonville.

In the early 1950s, many of Nannie's relatives died. In 1952 Arlie Lanning, her third husband, died at Lexington, North Carolina. Several months later, in 1953, her mother had a broken hip and Nannie nursed the woman who also died. In different towns, two of Nannie's sisters died the same year while she was visiting them. In 1953, Richard Morton (husband number four), was laid to rest at Emporia, Kansas.

In July 1954, Nannie married her fifth and last husband, Samuel Doss, in Tulsa, Oklahoma. Only a month later, he died, and the obligatory autopsy showed much arsenic.

ARREST AND TRIAL

In October 1954 Nannie Doss issued confessions covering three decades and at least ten murders. In 1955 she was sentenced to life imprisonment for the Tulsa case.

OUTCOME

She served ten years before succumbing to leukemia in 1965.

CHRISTINE FALLING

- ◊ **Date of birth:** March 12, 1963
- ◊ **Nickname:** Killer Babysitter
- ◊ **Motive:** She heard voices that made her kill the babies
- ◊ **Number of victims:** 6
- ◊ **Date of murders:** 1980-1982
- ◊ **Date of arrest:** July 1982
- ◊ **Murder method:** Suffocation
- ◊ **Known victims:** Children
- ◊ **Crime location:** Florida, USA
- ◊ **Status:** In December 1982 she was sentenced to life imprisonment

BACKGROUND

Christine Falling was born Christine Laverne Slaughter on March 12, 1963, in Perry, Florida.

At the time of her birth, Thomas, her father, was sixty-five while her mother Ann was just sixteen. They were a low-income family, and Christine did not have childhood support. She had epilepsy and was mentally lagging.

When Thomas and Ann could no longer support her, Christine spent some of her childhood and youth in orphanages. She compensated for her vulnerability and pent-up aggression by killing small animals, especially domestic cats, at an early age. She often caused the animals to fall from heights to test their "nine lives."

At the age of fourteen, in September 1977, her parents forced Christine to marry a 20-year-old Goober Falling. Only six weeks later, the marriage ended in divorce because of daily quarrels and violent fights. Christine fell ill. In 1978-1079 she went to the hospital fifty times for such reasons as hallucinations, "red spots" that appeared before her eyes and vaginal bleeding. When Christine was sixteen, doctors diagnosed her as disabled on medical instructions.

Falling began working as a babysitter for neighbors and friends to earn money.

MURDERS

On February 25, 1980, Christine Falling was babysitting for 2-year-old Cassidy Johnson. That day the baby felt worse, and doctors examined her at their office in Blountstown, Florida. They diagnosed her with meningitis caused by traumatic brain injuries. On February 28, the girl died from internal injuries. Christine explained that the child had fallen out of her crib. The physician did not believe the babysitter. He wrote a note with recommendations for police to check Falling; however, the record was lost on its way to the police department.

Christine Falling moved to Lakeland, Florida. While she was babysitting 4-year-old Jeffrey Davis, he died in the summer 1980. The autopsy revealed symptoms of myocarditis as the reason for death. Jeffrey's family attended his funeral and asked Falling to oversee his cousin. Two-year old Joseph Spring died a few hours later. Doctors diagnosed a viral infection.

In July 1981, Christine left Lakeland and returned to her hometown. She started to work as a nursing aide for the elderly. On the day when Falling began her work, 77-year-old William Swindle died in his kitchen.

In the fall of 1981, the daughter of Christine's half-sister, 8-month-old Jennifer Daniels died in the car. While the baby's mother had gone to the shopping center, she left her daughter with Christine for several minutes in the car, and the girl stopped breathing. Doctors suspected Sudden Infant Death Syndrome to be the cause of death.

On July 2, 1982, 10-week-old Travis Coleman died while Christine was taking care of him in Blountstown. At the autopsy, the doctors found internal injuries that could only have been caused by suffocation. When the police contacted Falling, she confessed to murdering the children, because she had heard voices ordering her, "Kill the baby." She had suffocated the children with pillows and blankets.

ARREST AND TRIAL

Christine Falling was arrested in July 1982 and sentenced to life in prison in December. Her confession prevented her from getting the death penalty.

After doing a stint of 25 years in prison, Falling was eligible for parole. In November 2017, the Parole Review Board rejected her application for parole. No one supporting her attended her parole hearing.

OUTCOME

Falling will be given another trial in seven years. She is imprisoned at a facility in Homestead, Florida.

LAVINIA FISHER

- ◇ **Date of birth:** 1793
- ◇ **Motive:** Robbery
- ◇ **Number of victims:** Not stated clearly
- ◇ **Date of murders:** 1818–1819
- ◇ **Date of arrest:** 1819
- ◇ **Murder method:** poisoning
- ◇ **Known victims:** lone travelers
- ◇ **Crime location:** Charleston, Charleston County, South Carolina, USA
- ◇ **Status:** On February 18, 1820, executed by hanging

BACKGROUND

Lavinia Fisher is reported to have been the first female serial killer in America. Not much is known about her origins; however, she lived much of her life in the United States. Her spouse was John Fisher. Some historians say that Lavinia Fisher did not kill anyone. Fisher was, however, an active member of a huge criminal group of highwaymen who operated out of two houses: The Five Mile House and the Six Mile House situated near Charleston. The outlaws hid at the Six Mile House; it is not clear whether it was a hotel.

Fisher and her spouse lived in Charleston, South Carolina. They owned a hotel, the Six Mile House, which they ran in the 19th century. The inn was six miles from Charleston. The local sheriff got messages that guests had disappeared. The claims came to nothing due to lack of evidence, and the popularity of the pair with the locals.

MURDERS

There were two versions of the murders. According to the first one, Lavinia Fisher invited lone travelers into the Six Mile House to have a meal and asked them about their occupations to find out if they had money. She brought a cup of poisoned tea to their rooms. When they were in bed, John checked to see if they were dead.

Another version was that the tea only put the men to sleep for a while. When they were asleep, Lavinia pulled a lever, and the bed dropped the victim into a deep hole. Some believed that there were spikes at the bottom of the pit.

In February 1819 a vigilante gang went

to the Fishers to stop the alleged "gang operations" that were arising in the area. After the group finished their task, they returned to Charleston but decided to leave David Ross as a guard there.

The next day, two men attacked him. Ross faced the gang that terrorized the region and saw Lavinia Fisher among them. She tried to choke him, but Ross escaped and alerted authorities.

Right after the incident, John Peeples, another lone traveler, asked Lavinia if there was a vacancy. She replied that there was no room, but he could come inside, and rest and have a cup of tea. Fortunately, John did not like tea. Lavinia questioned him for many hours, and after all, mentioned that they had a free room after all. He went to bed but felt suspicious about the questioning. John was afraid of being robbed and decided to sleep in a chair by the door. At midnight, he awoke to the loud sound of the bed dropping and jumped out the window. Immediately, John rode to Charleston to alert the authorities.

ARREST AND TRIAL

Police officers came to the location and arrested Lavinia and John along with two other gang members. John Fisher surrendered the group to protect his wife and shield her from possible gunfire.

Almost one year passed between the time of arrest and execution. At the accusation, the Fishers did not admit to being guilty, but they were jailed until their trial in May. The jury declined their statements of innocence and found them guilty of highway robbery, a serious crime.

The Fishers started to think about plans to escape, as they were at the South Carolina jail together and not well guarded. They put their ideas into action on September 13, but the rope they had made from prison bed linens tore, leaving Lavinia imprisoned and John set free. He did not want to continue the escape plan without his wife and he stayed in prison. The couple was then under more rigid security.

The Court sentenced Lavinia and John to be hanged on February 4, 1820. At that time Lavinia became sarcastic while John accepted the counsel of the Reverend Richard Furman.

OUTCOME

Lavinia reasoned to the judge that they could not hang a married woman, so they hanged John a day before.

CHARLENE GALLEGO

- ◊ **Date of birth:** October 10, 1956
- ◊ **Nickname:** Sex Slave Killer
- ◊ **Motive:** Sex
- ◊ **Number of victims:** 10
- ◊ **Date of murders:** September 11, 1978 – November 2, 1980
- ◊ **Date of arrest:** November 17, 1980
- ◊ **Murder method:** Her husband did the killing using blunt objects to crack the skull, guns, and strangulation
- ◊ **Known victims:** Runaways except for pregnant Mexican women, bartender, and young couple
- ◊ **Crime location:** California, Nevada, Oregon, the United States
- ◊ **Status:** Charlene completed her sentence in July 1997

BACKGROUND

Charlene Gallego was born Charlene Adell Williams in Stockton, California on 10 October 1956. She was a smart child from a supportive family. Her life changed when, as a young adult, she started using drugs and alcohol. She was married twice before meeting Gallego.

A Sacramento native she somehow fell head-over-heels for Gerald. Charlene learned to accept his quirks and fell into line with his fantasies to build a secret hideaway for holding "sex slaves" to do his bidding.

MURDERS

On 11 September 1978, 16-year-old Kippi Vaught and 17-year-old Rhonda Scheffler disappeared from Sacramento on the way to a local mall. Two days later the authorities found their ravaged and tattered bodies outside Baxter. Gerald had bound, beaten both girls with a tire iron, and fired a bullet through each one's skull.

Thirteen-year-old Sandra Colley and fourteen-year-old Brenda Judd vanished from the Washoe County Fairgrounds, in Reno, Nevada on June 24, 1979. Nobody saw the girls again, and both were listed as runaways until 1982 when Charlene Gallego's confession linked her husband with their murder.

On April 24, 1980, Stacey Redican and Karen Chipman disappeared from a Reno shopping center. On July 27, the police discovered their remains near Lovelock, Nevada. Gerald had sexually abused both girls, and then beat them to death with a blunt instrument.

Twenty-one-year-old Linda Aguilar was four months pregnant when she vanished on June 8, 1980, from Port Orford, Oregon. On June 20, Linda's relatives reported her missing. Several days later somebody found her body in a shallow grave located south of Gold Beach. Gerald shattered the victim's skull, bound her wrists and ankles with nylon cord, but an autopsy revealed sand in her nose, mouth, and throat, indicating that the Gallegos buried her alive.

Virginia Mochel, age 34, worked as a barmaid at a West Sacramento tavern. On July 17, 1980, the couple abducted her from the parking lot of her workplace. On October 30, Virginia's skeletal remains, bound with nylon fishing line, were found outside of Clarksburg, California.

On November 2, 1980, 22-year-old Craig Miller left a Sacramento fraternity dance with his date, 21-year-old Beth Sowers. Their friends could watch them in a car outside. A rough-looking stranger was sitting up front, on the passenger's side. Miller's friends memorized the license number. The next day they told their story to police when Craig was found dead near Bass Lake. Only three weeks later Beth Sowers was found, shot three times and dumped in a Placer County ditch.

ARREST AND TRIAL

Officers traced the car to Charlene's parents, recording their denial of the incident. She had secured a false identity by stealing a policeman's I.D. card. Gallego gave her name as "Mrs. Stephen Styles." Charlene's parents identified Gerald Gallego, and he fled the city. On November 3, Gerald used Charlene to phone home for money. Two weeks later, the next call came from Omaha. On November 17, federal agents were waiting when the couple called for their money at Western Union.

The killer team of man and wife did not plead guilty, but Charlene's attorneys convinced prosecutors to allow Charlene to testify against Gerald in return for a sentence of 16 years and eight months.

In June 1983 Gallego's trial in Sacramento, on charges of murdering Miller and Sowers, ended with his conviction and sentence of death in the gas chamber. In June 1984 the prosecutors found Gerald guilty of murder and kidnapping in the case of Karen Twiggs and Stacey Redican in Nevada, and they accordingly sentenced him to death.

OUTCOME

Charlene completed her sentence in July 1997. Gerald Gallego died of cancer in a Nevada prison medical center while awaiting execution in 2002.

JANIE LOU GIBBS

◊ **Date of birth:** December 25, 1932
◊ **Motive:** Life insurance money
◊ **Number of victims:** 5
◊ **Date of murders:** 1966–1967
◊ **Date of arrest:** 1967
◊ **Murder method:** Poisoning
◊ **Known victims:** her husband Marvin, her youngest son Marvin, her son Lester, her grandson Raymond, her son Robert
◊ **Crime location:** Georgia, United States
◊ **Status:** Died on February 7, 2010, at the age of 77 in Douglasville, Georgia

BACKGROUND

Janie Lou Gibbs married at the age of fifteen and became a grandmother at the age of thirty-four. Soft-spoken and bespectacled, she was eminent for her religious passion in Cordele, Georgia, where she worked steadily to be a "witness for the Lord." Gibbs taught Sunday school and served on numerous church committees. When not engaged in church work, Janie's particular pleasure was cooking for her family.

MURDERS

Gibbs committed her first crime in 1965. She poisoned her husband, Marvin, by putting rat poison in his dinner. While he was in a hospital, she cooked soup for him and put yet more arsenic into it. Doctors decided the cause of Marvin's death had been liver disease. The local church community supported her after her husband's death, and she donated some of her husband's life insurance money to the church.

Gibbs poisoned her youngest son Marvin eight months after her spouse's death. Doctors assumed he inherited a liver disease from his father. Janie again donated some of her life insurance money to the local church community.

Sixteen-year-old Lester, another of Gibbs's sons, died suddenly in January 1967. Doctors mentioned his cause of death as a muscular disorder.

Nineteen-year-old Robert was the only Gibbs son left. He had recently become father of a child named Raymond and Gibbs was happy to become a grandmother. It took a little time before Raymond became sick and died suddenly. His father followed him only a month later. The family physician became suspicious and referred the case to the state crime laboratory.

ARREST AND TRIAL

Robert's autopsy discovered that he had swallowed a lethal dose of arsenic. The local authorities exhumed the bodies of Gibbs' husband and three sons. On Christmas Day she was arrested for the crimes.

Medical experts found Gibbs mentally unfit to stand trial and confined her to a mental institution. Later she stood trial and prosecutors sentenced her to five life sentences.

In 1999 Gibbs was diagnosed with Parkinson's disease and was released into the custody of her sister.

OUTCOME

Gibbs died in 2010 in a nursing home in Douglasville, Georgia.

BERTHA GIFFORD

- ◊ **Date of birth:** October 1871
- ◊ **Number of victims:** 3–17
- ◊ **Date of murders:** 1900s–1928
- ◊ **Date of arrest:** 1928
- ◊ **Murder method:** Poisoning
- ◊ **Known victims:** Elmer and Lloyd Schamel, Edward Brinley
- ◊ **Crime location:** Catawissa, Missouri, United States
- ◊ **Status:** Committed to a mental facility where she remained until her death on August 20, 1951

BACKGROUND

Bertha Gifford was born in Grubville, Missouri, the daughter of William Poindexter Williams and his wife, Matilda. She was one of 10 children. Bertha was married to Henry Graham. Their union produced a daughter, Lila. She married Eugene Gifford following Graham's death. The couple had one child, James.

She had dark hair and complexion and was alleged to be one of the most beautiful women of Jefferson County.

Neighbors reported she was an extraordinary cook. They also said that Bertha was a friendly, caring woman who wore a white dress and carried her satchel to sick neighbors. However, many of her patients died violently, and the cause was "gastritis."

She also bought considerable amounts of arsenic for a rat infestation in her barn.

MURDERS

Mrs. Gifford was a tireless "Good Samaritan" and death-bed watcher. She was always ready to dash to the bedside of every dying neighbor who lived near her old farmhouse.

Bertha eagerly jumped out of her warm bed in the middle of the night, put on her nurse's uniform, which was always hanging on the chair, and hurried to the sick through any weather. Nothing could stop this woman, who usually got there ahead of the country doctor.

"Good old Bertha" really was a Good Samaritan provided her patients went through with the program of dying as expected. In that case, with prayers, tears, and tender ministrations, she eased their last moments, and she never asked money for her services.

The only trouble with Bertha was that when her patients rallied and gave promise of recovery, she rebelled against such attempts to cheat the grave and fed them rat poison.

Mrs. Gifford missed only one funeral in 18 years as she had a passion for death-beds and funerals. She also made funeral arrangements and liked to see everything done right.

Bertha was a very competent volunteer. Doctors knew her well. Mrs. Gifford understood symptoms and drugs.

She preferred little kids for her patients; this was because they fondly swallowed anything she gave them as it did not taste too nasty. Her small patients never presumed to correct any misstatement she might make to the doctor.

Mrs. Gifford usually turned to a mother and said in her kindly but firm professional manner to go to bed and have a good rest to take her place the next day.

The mother always obeyed her, relieved to know that her child was in more competent hands than her own.

Thus, Bertha had a whole night alone with the child. Next morning, she awoke the family, but the little patient would be gone. The nurse explained that health turned for the worse. Bertha wept harder than any of the parents or relatives.

Female neighbors first suspected Gifford. They put two and two together, and when Ed Brinley died, the seventeenth under Bertha's care, with the same symptoms, they required an investigation of this "saint." The authorities questioned the impressively indignant Bertha.

ARREST AND TRIAL

The last victim was Ed. Brinley, a neighbor, who rested for a fatal moment against the mailbox post, outside the Gifford house. Bertha's watchful eye spotted him there, and she ordered her husband to carry him in. When two hours later, he also died from the same symptoms; even the men admitted that it was suspicious.

The Grand Jury thought so too and indicted Bertha for murder, but she persisted in her denials until Andrew McConnell, chief of police took a hand. He noticed that the prisoner seemed especially annoyed at the suggestion that she had poisoned Beulah Mounds, the three-year-old daughter of S. Herman Pounds.

The police exhumed Brinley, Elmer and Lloyd Schamel, and their stomachs showed traces of arsenical poisoning. Bertha confessed and went to trial for their murders in Union, Missouri.

Gifford was found not guilty because of insanity and committed to the Missouri State Hospital #4.

OUTCOME

Bertha Gifford remained in a psychiatric institution until her death in 1951.

KRISTEN GILBERT

- ◇ **Date of birth:** November 13, 1967
- ◇ **Nickname:** The Angel of Death
- ◇ **Motive:** She wanted to attract attention, especially from her lover, a hospital security guard
- ◇ **Number of victims:** 4+
- ◇ **Date of murders:** 1995-1996
- ◇ **Date of arrest:** July 11, 1996
- ◇ **Murder method:** Poisoning (epinephrine)
- ◇ **Known victims:** Stanley Jagodowski, age 65; Henry Hudon, age 35; Kenneth Cutting, age 41; Edward Skwira, age 69
- ◇ **Crime location:** Massachusetts, United States
- ◇ **Status:** Sentenced to four life terms without the possibility of parole.

BACKGROUND

Kristen was the elder of Richard and Claudia Strickland's two daughters; Richard was an electronics executive; Claudia, a homemaker and part-time teacher.

In her teens, Gilbert had become a habitual liar. She enjoyed manipulating people and had a history of faking suicide attempts. Kristen has made violent threats against others since she was a teenager.

Gilbert graduated from high school at age sixteen, graduated from Greenfield Community College, and received licensure as a registered nurse in 1988. Later that year, she married Glenn Gilbert.

Kristen joined the staff of the Veterans Affairs Medical Center in Northampton in 1989. She distinguished herself early on and was featured in the magazine VA Practitioner in April 1990.

MURDERS

Other nurses, however, observed many deaths on Gilbert's watch. Her colleagues decided not to pay attention to this, and playfully called Kristen the "Angel of Death."

In 1996, three nurses informed the chief physician about a decrease in the supply of epinephrine and an increase in cardiac arrest deaths. An investigation followed. Gilbert attempted to derail the investigation and phoned in a bomb threat.

Staff at the VAMC had speculated that she intended to demonstrate her nursing skills by creating emergencies. Others claim that she was using these emergencies to gain the attention of James Perrault's, a VA police officer. He later had an affair with Gilbert. VA hospital rules required that hospital police be present at any medical emergency.

ARREST AND TRIAL

In 1996 Gilbert left the hospital amid a hospital investigation into the many suspicious patient deaths that occurred during her working shifts.

VA hospital staff members speculated that Gilbert might have been responsible for eighty or more deaths and more than three hundred medical emergencies.

Officer Perrault witnessed against Kristen. He said that she confessed at least one murder to him by phone.

A state jury convicted Gilbert on three counts of first-degree murder, one count of second-degree murder on March 14, 2001.

The jury suggested a sentence of life imprisonment on March 26, 2001. On March 27, the judge sentenced Gilbert to four life terms without the possibility of parole.

They transferred Kristen Gilbert to a special federal prison in Texas from a prison for women in Framingham, Massachusetts.

OUTCOME

Gilbert is serving her sentence at a Federal Medical Center, Carswell in Fort Worth, Texas.

HELEN GOLAY AND OLGA RUTTERSCHMIDT

- ◊ **Date of birth:** 1930 (Golay) and 1933 (Rutterschmidt)
- ◊ **Nicknames:** Black Widows
- ◊ **Motive:** Life insurance policies
- ◊ **Number of victims:** 2
- ◊ **Date of murders:** 1999, 2005
- ◊ **Date of arrest:** 2008
- ◊ **Murder method:** Hit-and-run
- ◊ **Known victims:** Paul Vados and Kenneth McDavid
- ◊ **Crime location:** California, United States
- ◊ **Status:** Both sentenced to consecutive life term.

BACKGROUND

Olga Rutterschmidt was born in Hungary, 1933. In 1957, she emigrated to the United States and owned a coffee shop in Los Angeles with her husband. In the 1970s, having divorced, she moved to Hollywood.

MURDERS

On November 8, 1999, seventy-three-year-old homeless man Paul Vados was found dead in an alley near 307 North La Brea Avenue in Hollywood, California. Vados had emigrated from Hungary in 1956. He appeared to be the victim of a hit-and-run.

Two years before, in 1997, Rutterschmidt and her murder partner, Helen Golay, applied for life insurance policies on Vados. They listed themselves as beneficiaries. After Vados's death, Rutterschmidt and Golay received benefits from eight different life insurance policies that had been taken out on him.

On June 21, 2005, according to a surveillance video, fifty-year-old homeless man Kenneth McDavid was hit by a silver Mercury Sable station wagon. He was originally from northern California and had attended Sacramento State University.

From 2002 to 2003, Golay and Rutterschmidt took out a total of thirteen policies on McDavid. On different insurance applications, Rutterschmidt and Golay were mentioned as McDavid's business partner, fiancé or cousin.

Before her arrest, Rutterschmidt had received a total of $674,571.89 in insurance proceeds from McDavid's death.

ARREST AND TRIAL

A 48-year-old homeless man, Jimmy Covington, testified at trial that Rutterschmidt had approached him, took him to Burger King and promised him shelter. Covington stated that he had moved out after growing suspicious when Golay and Rutterschmidt asked him to sign documents and give his details to them. Rutterschmidt and Golay had already filled out a life insurance policy application for him.

When Rutterschmidt and Golay were in jail, the prosecutors secretly recorded their conversations. Rutterschmidt told Golay in one conversation that the latter did all those insurances extra, and that was what raised the suspicion. In fact, the suspicion had been raised when a detective overheard a colleague discussing a similar case.

In April 2008, both Rutterschmidt and Golay were convicted in Los Angeles, California, of conspiracy to the first-degree murder of Vados and McDavid. The trial judge sentenced both women to consecutive life terms in California Federal prison, without the possibility of parole.

The Court of Appeal, Second District, State of California denied appeals to the convictions and sentences on August 18, 2009. The California Supreme Court also rejected the appeals on October 28, 2012.

MEDIA

On February 10, 2010, CNBC broadcasted "The Black Widow Murders" on an episode of American Greed. On September 10, 2009, the case was featured on a "Behind the Mask" episode of Deadly Women. The same year, the series Wicked Attraction featured a "Golden Years" episode in its second season detailing criminal acts and the history of the two. On November 13, 2013, Elder Skelter profiled a story about Ken McDavid's death. The episode was called "Death, Lies and Security Tape."

On December 16, 2009, CSI: NY aired the episode "Second Chances" which mirrors a great deal of the Black Widow Murders, but with a younger cast, consisting of Kim Kardashian and Vanessa Minnillo as the money-hungry black widows.

GWENDOLYN GRAHAM AND CATHY WOOD

- ◊ **Date of birth:** August 6, 1963 (Graham); March 7, 1962 (Wood)
- ◊ **Nicknames:** The Lethal Lovers
- ◊ **Motive:** The secret of a murder would cement their bond
- ◊ **Number of victims:** 5
- ◊ **Date of murders:** January – February 1987
- ◊ **Date of arrest:** December 1988
- ◊ **Murder method:** Smothering
- ◊ **Known victims:** Elderly female patients
- ◊ **Crime location:** Michigan, US
- ◊ **Status:** Sentenced to life in prison without the possibility of parole.

BACKGROUND

In 1987 Gwendolyn Graham and Catherine May Wood were a twenty-four-year-old and twenty-five-year-old lesbian couple from Grand Rapids, Michigan. They worked at a nursing home and achieved sexual thrills by killing five elderly female patients. Together they would smother their victims and make love shortly after that to relive and enhance their lovemaking. Catherine Wood was a massive four-hundred-fifty-pound woman who intensely loved the more dominant Gwendolyn Graham who liked sexual experimentation. When Gwendolyn decided to leave to take a new job in Texas, Catherine broke down and confessed to authorities. Wood got twenty years in prison, and Graham received a penalty of life imprisonment.

MURDERS

Graham killed a few senior women posting Wood as a lookout. However, women could fight back. In January 1987, Graham murdered a woman who had Alzheimer's disease. The woman was too disabled to fight back, and thus became the pair's first victim. The woman's death seemed to be natural, so there was no autopsy.

Graham and Wood killed four more Alpine Manor patients over the next few months. Many of the victims, aged from sixty-five to ninety-seven, were disabled because of Alzheimer's disease. Graham and Wood played a game, choosing victims when their initials jointly spelled M-U-R-D-E-R. Graham took memorable souvenirs from her victims.

Both women openly boasted to their colleagues about smothering six victims. Graham even showed off her souvenirs, but no one believed her.

The pair broke up when Wood refused to kill a patient to prove her love for Graham. Wood transferred to another working shift. Graham moved to Texas with another woman and began work in a hospital taking care of infants.

ARREST AND TRIAL

In October 1998 Wood's ex-husband went to the police, and the murder investigation began. On November 30, 1988, the police exhumed the first victim almost a year after the burial.

The police identified eight possible victims, but they pursued five.

The authorities had enough evidence to arrest both Wood and Graham. The police arrested the latter in December 1989, in her hometown of Tyler, Texas; however, Graham maintained their statements were made as a joke to frighten their colleagues.

During the litigation, Wood admitted her guilt, claiming she just distracted supervisors or served as a lookout for Graham. Wood stated it was Graham who planned and carried out the killings.

The court found Graham guilty on November 3, 1989, and gave her five life sentences. The court gave Wood twenty years on one count of second-degree murder and one count of conspiracy to commit second-degree murder. Since March 2, 2005, she has been eligible for parole.

OUTCOME

Graham resides in the Huron Valley Complex. Wood is expected to be released on June 6, 2021, from the minimum security Federal Correctional Institution in Tallahassee, Florida.

DANA SUE GRAY

- ◇ **Date of birth:** December 6, 1957
- ◇ **Motive:** Robbery
- ◇ **Number of victims:** 3 (murder), 1 (robbery and attempted murder)
- ◇ **Date of murders:** February 16, 1994–March 16, 1994
- ◇ **Date of arrest:** March 16, 1994
- ◇ **Murder method:** Stabbing with knife and ligature strangulation
- ◇ **Known victims:** Norma Davis, 86; June Roberts, 66; Dora Beebe, 87
- ◇ **Crime location:** California, The United States
- ◇ **Status:** On October 16, 1998, sentenced to life in prison without parole

BACKGROUND

On December 6, 1957, Dana Sue Gray was born Dana Sue Armbrust in southern California. Her parents were Russell Armbrust and Beverly Armbrust (née Arnett). Russell worked as a hairdresser and had three marriages before marrying Beverly. During her teens, she was a beauty queen. Beverly had several miscarriages before Dana was born. Russel and Beverly divorced when he found her grappling with an older woman who had angered her. Beverly was an aggressive, vain woman who regularly maxed out her husband's credit cards. At the time Dana was two years old and rarely saw her beloved father. She started to act out to get attention. When Beverly tried to discipline her, Dana would steal money to buy candy and would periodically become furious. She was not friends with other students in school and did not study. Dana Sue forged notes to get out of class and was suspended from school many times.

When Dana was 14, doctors diagnosed her mother's breast cancer. Gray watched hospital nurses treat her mother and decided to become a nurse. Soon Gray's mother died, and she moved in with her father; however, both her stepmother and father forced her to leave when they found drugs in her room. Several years later, Gray became involved with a skydiving instructor. He got her pregnant twice but convinced her to abort both pregnancies, something she resented.

Gray married a man named William

L. Gray in October 1987 at a winery in the Temecula area. Gray was a fellow sports enthusiast who had known and admired her since high school. Dana was a serious athlete, very fit, and beautiful with blonde hair. Their marriage quickly got into trouble when Dana drove them into debt.

The Grays lived in the gated community of Canyon Lake where they had several business ventures under the name Graymatter. In early 1993 Dana left her husband and moved in with their friend and her lover, Jim Wilkins. She filed for divorce from Gray in June 1993.

On February 14, 1994, Dana Sue sent word through Gray's parents that she wanted to meet with her alienated husband. Gray agreed but did not come. Later that day, Dana Gray murdered an elderly lady named Norma Davis.

MURDERS

N orma Davis, 86, was Dana's first victim. However, Gray never confessed to the murder. She knew Norma very well as the latter was the mother-in-law of the woman (Jeri) who married Gray's father in 1988. Bill Davis, Jeri's first husband, was Norma's son. Jeri did not stop caring for her elderly mother-in-law, even after she remarried.

On February 16, 1994, Alice Williams, Norma Davis's neighbor, found her dead with a utility knife protruding from her neck, and a fillet knife protruding from her chest. Detectives figured that there was no forced entry into the house. Neighbors informed detectives that she constantly kept the door locked unless she was waiting for a visitor. Alice Williams stated she did not remember Davis mentioning she was expecting company.

On February 28, 1994, Gray killed sixty-six-year-old June Roberts who lived in the gated community of Canyon Lake. Gray had visited Roberts one day. Dana told June she wanted to borrow a book about controlling a drinking problem. Roberts let Gray into her house. While June searched for the book, Gray unplugged Roberts' phone; both the straight cord and the curly cord were used to strangle Roberts. When Roberts was dead, Gray rummaged through her credit cards, stealing two. One hour later, Gray went on a massive shopping spree at a shopping center in Temecula.

Dana Sue Gray attacked fifty-seven-year-old Hawkins at her job at an antique store. That day Hawkins had been working alone. Dana came in to buy a picture frame for a photo of her deceased mother. Gray used a telephone cord to strangle Hawkins. Gray took $20 from the cash register and $5 from Hawkins' purse. Only one hour later, Gray used Roberts' credit card and went on another shopping spree. Hawkins had survived the assault and was able to give detectives a description of Gray.

On March 16, 1994, Gray killed eighty-seven-year-old Dora Beebe. Several minutes after Beebe came home from a doctor's appointment, Gray knocked on her door and asked for directions. Beebe let Gray inside to look at a map. Once inside Gray attacked and killed Beebe. Louis Dormand, Beebe's boyfriend, found her later that day. The same day, Gray also used Beebe's credit card to go on a shopping spree.

ARREST AND TRIAL

Police finally caught Gray because various merchants described her. Dana spent a vast amount of money, and the credit card company called June Roberts' family to warn them of the massive spending. The police officers then went to all the shopping centers where Gray used the credit cards. The detectives interviewed the cashiers and got a physical description of the killer. They also discovered the murderer had dyed her hair lately and had a little boy named Jason. Detective Greco stayed in touch with Jeri Armbrust. He visited her and described the killer. The next day Jeri revealed to Greco that the suspect was Dana Gray, her stepdaughter, who had recently dyed her hair and had a boyfriend with a son named Jason. The detective wrote a search warrant for Gray's home.

The detectives saw Dana go to the bank with Beebe's card and then go shopping, so they had enough evidence for Dora Beebe's murder. Detective Greco arrested Dana later that day. He took her into custody while police officers took her boyfriend and his son for questioning.

Gray claimed she found both Roberts' and Beebe's credit cards. Detective Greco finally booked Gray on charges of murder. Deputy DA Richard Bentley queried the death penalty at a hearing on July 23. Gray appealed insanity on all counts. A witness declared to have seen Gray at Roberts' house the day of her death. Gray had nothing to do but change her plea to guilty of robbing and murdering two women and attempting to murder another. By pleading guilty Gray escaped the death penalty.

OUTCOME

Dana Gray was sentenced to life without parole in the California Women's Prison in Chowchilla on October 16, 1998.

BELLE GUNNESS

- ◊ **Date of birth:** November 11, 1859
- ◊ **Nicknames:** Hell's Belle, the Black Widow, Lady Bluebeard
- ◊ **Motive:** Money, evading capture
- ◊ **Number of victims:** 25 – 40
- ◊ **Date of murders:** 1884 – 1908
- ◊ **Date of arrest:** Never caught
- ◊ **Murder method:** Poisoning (strychnine), bludgeoning
- ◊ **Known victims:** Men and children
- ◊ **Crime location:** Illinois, Indiana, USA
- ◊ **Status:** The bodies of Gunness' children were found in the home's wreckage on April 28, 1908, but the headless adult female corpse found with them was never identified.

BACKGROUND

Belle Gunness was born Brynhild Paulsdatter Strseth on November 22, 1859, in Selbu, Norway. Her parents were Paul Pedersen Størset and Berit Olsdatter. Belle was the youngest of the couple's eight children. They lived at a very small cotter's farm in Innbygda, 60 km southeast of Trondheim, the largest city in central Norway. The daughter of a stonemason, she immigrated to America in 1881 in search of wealth.

Standing six feet tall (183 cm) and weighing over 200 pounds (91 kg), Belle was a physically strong woman.

Gunness married Mads Albert Sorenson in 1884. Not long after the marriage, their store and home mysteriously burned down. The pair got the insurance money for both buildings. Soon afterward, Sorenson died of heart failure on the day his two life insurance policies overlapped. Though her husband's family demanded an inquiry, the police filed no charges. It was thought the couple had two children.

MURDERS

Gunness poisoned her two children for the insurance money in infancy.

Several more deaths followed, including her new husband's infant daughter. Peter Gunness followed his little daughter. Belle had an adopted daughter, Jennie, whose body would also be found on Gunness's property.

Belle Gunness began dating wealthy men through a lovelorn column. Her next victims were her suitors. They brought money to her farm and then disappeared forever.

In 1908 Gunness's luck seemed to be running out; her farmhouse burned. Workers found four skeletons in the smoldering ruins. Three were identified as her adoptive children. The fourth, believed to be Gunness, was missing the skull. The remains of men and children were unearthed from graves around the farm. More than forty were discovered.

ARREST AND TRIAL

Gunness had never been arrested. On May 22, 1908, the police arrested Gunness's hired hand, Ray Lamphere, for murder and arson. He later stated that Gunness ordered him to burn her farmhouse to the ground with her children inside. Ray also declared that the body believed to be Belle's was one of her victims.

OUTCOME

Gunness planned the crime to mislead investigators. Having withdrawn most of her money from bank accounts, she skipped town. Nobody saw her again, and nobody could confirm her death.

ANNA MARIE HAHN

- ◊ **Date of birth:** July 7, 1906
- ◊ **Nicknames:** Marie Felser, Marie Fisher, Arsenic Anna, The Blonde Borgia, Angel of Mercy
- ◊ **Motive:** To support her gambling habit
- ◊ **Number of victims:** 5
- ◊ **Date of murders:** May 6, 1933 – August 1, 1937
- ◊ **Date of arrest:** 1937
- ◊ **Murder method:** Poisoning (arsenic)
- ◊ **Known victims:** Ernest Koch, 73; Albert Parker, 72; Jacob Wagner, 78; George Gsellman, 67; George Obendoerfer, 67
- ◊ **Crime location:** Ohio, United States
- ◊ **Status:** Executed at the Ohio Penitentiary by electrocution.

BACKGROUND

Anna Hahn's family had twelve children, and she was the youngest. In her teens, she had an affair with a Viennese physician. Their relationship produced a son named Oskar. In 1929 Hahn's scandalized family sent her to the U.S., while her son remained with her parents in Bavaria. Hahn met fellow German immigrant Philip Hahn while staying with relatives Max and Anna Doeschel in Cincinnati, Ohio. They married in 1930. Hahn briefly returned to Germany to retrieve Oscar, and they began life as a family with Philip.

MURDERS

Hahn began poisoning and robbing senior men and women in Cincinnati's German community to support her gambling habit. Her first victim was Ernst Kohler, who died on May 6, 1933. Kohler left her a house in his will.

Her next victim, seventy-two-year-old Albert Parker, died soon after she began caring for him. Before Parker's death, she borrowed $1,000 from him, but after his death, the I.O.U. "disappeared."

On June 3, 1937, seventy-eight-year-old Jacob Wagner died, leaving $17,000 to his niece, Hahn.

She soon began caring for sixty-seven-year-old George Gsellman. On July 6, 1937, before his death, she received $15,000 in cash for her service.

On August 1, 1937, Georg Obendoerfer

traveled to Colorado Springs with Hahn and her son. He was the last to die. Police conducted an autopsy, which revealed high levels of arsenic in Obendoerfer's body. The exhumation showed that two of her previous clients had also been poisoned.

ARREST AND TRIAL

In November 1937, after a sensational four-week trial the judge convicted Hahn. On December 7, 1938, sentenced to death, she went to the electric chair at the Ohio Penitentiary in Columbus.

OUTCOME

Hahn was buried in Mount Calvary Cemetery in Columbus.

LIZZIE HALLIDAY

- ◊ **Date of birth:** c. 1859
- ◊ **Motive:** Insurance money
- ◊ **Number of victims:** 4
- ◊ **Date of murders:** 1890s
- ◊ **Date of arrest:** 1893
- ◊ **Murder method:** Poisoning (arsenic) and shooting
- ◊ **Known victims:** Her husbands and a son
- ◊ **Crime location:** New York, United States
- ◊ **Status:** died on June 28, 1918

BACKGROUND

Lizzie Halliday was born Eliza Margaret McNally around 1859 in County Antrim, Ireland. When she was a young girl, her family moved to the US. Lizzie married a Pennsylvania man named Charles Hopkins in 1879. They had a son who was institutionalized. After Hopkins' death, in 1881, she married a pensioner, Artemus Brewer. Less than a year later, he also died. Her third husband, named Hiram Parkinson, left her within their first year of marriage. Lizzie then married George Smith, who was a war veteran and had served with Brewer. After a failed attempt to kill Smith by adding arsenic in his tea, Lizzie escaped to Bellows Falls, Vermont. She married Charles Playstel from Vermont and vanished two weeks later.

In 1888, Lizzie returned to Philadelphia. People saw her at a saloon on 1218 North Front Street. The McQuillans, friends she knew from Ireland, ran that saloon. Going by the name "Maggie Hopkins," Lizzie set up a shop but was later convicted of burning it down for the insurance money. She was sentenced to two years at Philadelphia's Eastern State Penitentiary.

Under the name "Lizzie Brown," she became the housekeeper for Paul Halliday in 1889. He was a twice-widowed seventy-year-old farmer from Burlingham, New York with his sons. Their marriage was darkened by what Halliday described as Lizzie's sporadic "spells of insanity." The Halliday family's house and barn burned down, and the authorities suspected Lizzie of setting the fires.

MURDERS

In May 1893, the Halliday mill barn burned with Halliday's mentally ill son John inside. Lizzie disliked John, and the police suspected her of setting the fire. The officers arrested her and sent her to an asylum, but the doctors declared Lizzie cured, and she returned home to Halliday.

In August 1893, Halliday disappeared again. Lizzie claimed he had gone to a neighboring town to work. Some neighbors told the police about their suspicions that something was wrong with Lizzie's story. The police officers obtained a search warrant and found the bodies of two women buried in the hay in a barn on September 4. The women were Margaret and Sarah McQuillan. Lizzie shot both. When officers questioned Lizzie, she behaved in an unstable manner.

ARREST AND TRIAL

The police discovered Paul Halliday's mutilated body under the flooring of his house. Lizzie shot him too. She was accused of the crimes and held for trial at the Sullivan County jail in New York. During her first few months in prison, Lizzie refused to eat, attacked the sheriff's wife, and set fire to her bed. She also tried to hang herself and cut her own throat with broken glass. Her jailers chained her to the floor during her remaining months there.

On June 21, 1894, the judge convicted Lizzie Halliday for the murder of McQuillans at the Sullivan County Oyer and Terminer Court. Halliday was the first woman ever to be sentenced to death by electrocution, via New York State's new electric chair, but after a medical commission declared her insane, Governor Roswell P. Flower commuted her sentence to life in a mental institution. They sent Halliday to the Matteawan State Hospital for the Criminally Insane. She spent the rest of her life there. In 1906, she killed a nurse, Nellie Wickes, by stabbing her two hundred times with a pair of scissors.

OUTCOME

Lizzie Halliday died on June 28, 1918.

LINDA HAZZARD

- ◊ **Date of birth:** December 18, 1867
- ◊ **Motive:** To cure diseases
- ◊ **Number of victims:** 40+
- ◊ **Date of murders:** 1908 – 1911
- ◊ **Date of arrest:** August 1911
- ◊ **Murder method:** Starvation
- ◊ **Known victims:** Mrs. Elgin Cox; Daisey Maud Haglund, Ida Wilcox; Blanche B. Tindall; Viola Heaton; Eugene Stanley Wakelin
- ◊ **Crime location:** Olalla, Kitsap County, Washington, United States
- ◊ **Status:** She died of self-starvation in 1938.

BACKGROUND

Linda Hazzard, born Lynda Laura Burfield in Carver, Minnesota, was one of eight children born to Montgomery and Susanna Neil Burfield. Linda had no medical degree but had a license to practice medicine in Washington. According to her book The Science of Fasting, she studied under Edward Hooker Dewey, a champion of fasting.

MURDERS

She established a sanitarium, Wilderness Heights, in Washington. Her patients fasted for days, weeks, or months on a diet. They drank small amounts of asparagus and tomato juice and occasionally a tiny teaspoon of orange juice. Some patients survived and sang her praises, but more than forty patients died under Linda's care. Hazzard stated that they all died of hidden or undiagnosed illnesses such as cirrhosis of the liver or cancer. Her opponents asserted that they all died of starvation. Local people referred to the sanitarium as "Starvation Heights." Linda assured people that her approach was a panacea for all ills because she could rid the body of toxins and impurities that caused imbalances in the body.

During her medical career, Hazzard wrote two books about the science behind fasting, and how it could cure illnesses. In 1908 she wrote the first book Fasting for the Cure of Disease. In 1927 Hazzard wrote the second book Scientific Fasting: The Ancient and Modern Key to Health.

ARREST AND TRIAL

In 1912, the judge convicted her of the unpremeditated murder of Claire Williamson, a wealthy British woman, who weighed less than fifty pounds at the time of her death. During the trial, prosecutors proved that Hazzard had falsified Williamson's will and stolen most of her valuables. Dorothea, Williamson's sister, also took the treatment and only survived because a family friend insisted on removing her from that place. Dorothea could not leave on her own because she was too weak, weighing less than sixty pounds. At trial, she witnessed against Hazzard.

The officials sentenced Hazzard to twenty-two years in prison, which she served in the Washington State Penitentiary in Walla Walla. On December 26, 1915, Hazzard was released on parole after serving two years. She and her husband, Samuel Chrisman Hazzard, moved to New Zealand, where she practiced as a dietitian and osteopath until 1920.

She returned to Olalla, Washington in 1920 and opened a new sanitarium since her medical license had been revoked. Hazzard continued to supervise fasts until it burned down in 1935.

OUTCOME

In 1938, Linda Burfield Hazzard died while attempting a fasting cure on herself.

AUDREY MARIE HILLEY

- ◊ **Date of birth:** June 4, 1933
- ◊ **Motive:** Insurance money
- ◊ **Number of victims:** 1
- ◊ **Date of murders:** May 25, 1975
- ◊ **Date of arrest:** October 1979/ January 1983
- ◊ **Murder method:** Poisoning (arsenic)
- ◊ **Known victims:** Her husband, Frank Hilley
- ◊ **Crime location:** Anniston, Calhoun County, Alabama, United States
- ◊ **Status:** Died from hypothermia on February 26, 1987

BACKGROUND AND CRIMES

Audrey Marie Hilley was born Audrey Marie Frazier on June 4, 1933, in Blue Mountain, Alabama to Lucille and Huey Frazier.

In May 1951, she married Frank Hilley, who later, in May 1975, visited his doctor complaining of tenderness in his abdomen and nausea. The doctor diagnosed him with a viral stomachache. He went to a hospital for tests that indicated a liver malfunction. Therapists then diagnosed him with infectious hepatitis. He passed away on May 25, 1975.

Audrey Hilley gave her permission for performing an autopsy. It revealed swelling of the kidneys and lungs, bilateral pneumonia, and inflammation of the stomach. Physicians did not conduct tests for poison because the symptoms closely resembled those of hepatitis. The doctors indicated infectious hepatitis as a cause of death.

Frank Hilley had maintained a life insurance policy that his widow redeemed for $31,140. She took out her daughter's $25,000 life insurance policy three years later.

Within several months, Carol began to suffer from nausea. After insuring her daughter, Hilley gave her an injection that she said would relieve nausea. The symptoms did not disappear but worsened. Carol began to experience numbness in her limbs. Carol's physician conducted some tests but was unable to diagnose any disease and called for a psychiatrist because he thought the symptoms might be psychosomatic. While Carol was undergoing psychiatric testing, she received two more injections from her mother. Audrey explained that the doses were given to her by a friend who was a registered nurse.

Carol's physician conducted a few more tests and began to suspect heavy metal poisoning was the cause for the symptoms.

The same day, Hilley had Carol discharged from the hospital. She was taken to the University of Alabama Hospital in Birmingham the next day. Coincidentally, the police arrested Hilley for passing bad checks, which she had written to the insurance company that insured Carol's life. It caused that policy to lapse.

The university hospital physicians focused on the possibility of Carol's heavy metal poisoning, noting that her hands and feet were numb. Carol also had nerve palsy, causing foot drop, and she had lost most of her deep tendon reflexes.

ARREST AND TRIAL

Finally, physicians discovered Aldrich-Mees' lines in Carol's fingernails and toenails, an indicator of arsenic poisoning.

Doctors conducted tests on samples of Carol's hair, which revealed that it had about 50 times the average arsenic level in human hair. Physicians then officially attributed her condition to arsenic poisoning.

The police then had suspicions and exhumed Frank Hilley's body for testing. The analysis showed unnaturally high levels of arsenic, ranging from ten times the normal level in hair samples to a hundred times the normal level

in toenail samples. Dr. Joseph Embry concluded that acute arsenic poisoning was the cause of death.

On October 9, 1979, the officers arrested Audrey Hilley for the attempted murder of her daughter. The police found another bottle in her purse, and further testing detected the presence of arsenic.

On November 9, 1979, the authorities released Audrey Hilley on bond. She disappeared, leaving a note indicating that she "might have been kidnapped." The police filed a missing person report and listed Audrey as a fugitive.

On January 11, 1980, the police indicted Audrey in absentia for her husband's murder. Investigators discovered that both her mother and her mother-in-law had considerable traces of arsenic in their bodies when they died.

Although the FBI and police launched a massive search, Hilley remained a fugitive for three years.

Under the name Robbi Hannon, she traveled to Florida, where she met a man named John Homan. In May 1981 she married Homan and took his last name. They moved to New Hampshire. She regularly talked about her imaginary twin sister, "Teri," who allegedly lived in Texas.

In 1982, Audrey left New Hampshire, telling her husband that she needed to see doctors about an illness.

During the trip, using the assumed name Teri Martin, she called her husband and told him that his wife had died in Texas. She had donated her "sister's" body to medical science, so there was no need for him to come.

She changed her hair color, lost weight, and returned to New Hampshire to meet John Homan, posing as Teri Martin, his "gone" wife's sister.

A New Hampshire newspaper published an obituary for Robbi Homan, but the police were unable to confirm any of the information it set forth. A police detective supposed that the woman living as Teri Martin was Robbi Homan who had staged the death. That hunch bore fruit, and after police brought "Teri Martin" in for questioning, "Robbi" confessed to being Audrey Marie Hilley. The police returned her to Alabama to face trial.

The judge quickly convicted her and sentenced her to life in prison for her husband's murder and twenty years for attempting to kill her daughter.

OUTCOME

In 1983 she began serving her sentence and was a quiet prisoner. John Homan had moved to Anniston to be near his wife. In February 1987, the officials gave Hilley a three-day pass to visit her husband. The couple spent a day at a motel, and when John left for a few hours, she escaped, leaving behind a note asking his forgiveness.

Hilley did not stay missing very long. Four days after she disappeared, Anniston police went to a home and caught her. She had been creeping around in the woods, soaked by four days of rain and numb from temperatures dropping to the low 30s.

The police officers took Audrey to a local hospital where she suffered heart failure and died.

WANETA HOYT

- ◊ **Date of birth:** May 13, 1946
- ◊ **Motive:** Unwanted children and spousal revenge
- ◊ **Number of victims:** 5
- ◊ **Date of murders:** 1965 – 1971
- ◊ **Date of arrest:** March 23, 1994
- ◊ **Murder method:** Suffocation
- ◊ **Known victims:** Her biological children: Erik (3 months, 10 days old); Julie (1 month, 17 days old); James (2 years, 4 months old); Molly (2 months, 18 days old); Noah (2 months, 19 days old)
- ◊ **Crime location:** Oswego, Oswego County, New York, United States
- ◊ **Status:** Died in prison on August 13, 1998

BACKGROUND

Waneta Ethel Hoyt was born in Richford, New York. In the 10th grade, she dropped out of Newark Valley High School and married Tim Hoyt on January 11, 1964. She suffered from measles that left her with poor eyesight, and without glasses, she could only see shadows.

MURDERS

The couple's son Eric died on January 26, 1965, only 101 days after he was born on October 17, 1964. None of their other children – James (May 31, 1966 – September 26, 1968), Julie (July 19 – September 5, 1968), Molly (March 18 – June 5, 1970), and Noah (May 9 – July 28, 1971) survived. For over twenty years, everybody thought that the babies had died of sudden infant death syndrome. Not so many years after the death of their last child, Mr. and Mrs. Hoyt adopted a child, Jay. He remained healthy through childhood and was 17 years old when the police arrested Mrs. Hoyt in 1994.

The last two Hoyt children, Molly and Noah, were subjects of pediatric research. Dr. Alfred Steinschneider conducted it and published an article in 1972 in the Journal of Pediatrics proposing a connection between sleep apnea and SIDS. The report was controversial.

ARREST AND TRIAL

In 1985 one of the experts, Dr. Linda Norton, a forensic pathologist from Dallas, believed that there might be a serial killer in that area of New York. She suspected this after reading

Steinschneider's article on the Hoyt case. Dr. Norton told her suspicions to a prosecutor from a neighboring county. He had been dealing with a murder case that was initially thought to involve SIDS.

In 1992, when the prosecutor became District Attorney, he sent the case to forensic pathologist Michael Baden for analysis. Baden concluded that the fatalities were the result of murder.

In 1994, the authorities transferred the case to the District Attorney of the county where the Hoyts lived. In March 1994 a New York State trooper, with whom Hoyt was acquainted, asked her for help in research on SIDS, and she agreed. The policeman questioned her, and at the end of the inquiry, she confessed to the murders of her five biological children by suffocation. Consequently, she was arrested. The reason she gave for the killings was that the babies were crying, and she wanted to silence them.

OUTCOME

The judge sentenced Hoyt to 75 years to life on September 11, 1995. In August 1998, Hoyt died in prison of pancreatic cancer.

MARTHA ANN JOHNSON

- ◊ **Date of birth:** 1955
- ◊ **Other names:** Martha Ann Bowen
- ◊ **Motive:** To punish her husband
- ◊ **Number of victims:** 4
- ◊ **Date of murders:** 1977 – 1982
- ◊ **Date of arrest:** July 3, 1989
- ◊ **Murder method:** Smothering
- ◊ **Known victims:** Her children: James William Taylor, 23-month-old; Tabitha Jenelle Bowen, 3-month-old; Earl Wayne Bowen, 31-month-old; Jenny Ann Wright, 11-year-old
- ◊ **Crime location:** Clayton County, Georgia, United States
- ◊ **Status:** On May 1990, sentenced to life in prison

BACKGROUND

Born in 1955, a Georgia native, Martha Johnson, was married for the third time at age twenty-two. The first marriage had produced a daughter, Jennyann Wright, born in 1971. James William Taylor, the product of Martha's second marriage, followed in 1975. Husband number three, Earl Bowen, got along well with Martha's children and fathered two of his own – Earl Wayne in 1979 and Tabitha Janel in 1980, but he did not get along with Martha.

The couple argued bitterly, and Earl repeatedly walked out to let his temper cool. They always patched things up, but Martha had begun to feel the strain. Perhaps she saw the children as a stumbling block to happiness or they were pawns in a deadly private game. In either case, the result was lethal.

MURDERS

On September 23, 1977, Johnson declared her son James William Taylor, aged 23 months, was unresponsive when she strove to rouse him from his nap. The ambulance rushed the child to the hospital, but paramedics could do nothing and pronounced him dead. The physicians determined the cause of death was sudden infant death syndrome (SIDS).

On November 30, 1980, Johnson claimed her daughter Tabitha Jenelle Bowen, aged three months, was blue when she tried to wake her from a nap. Doctors could not revive the baby and attributed Tabitha's death to SIDS.

In January 1981, Earl Wayne Bowen, aged 31 months, was found with a pack of rat poison. Doctors treated him and released him from the hospital. In some days Earl's parents declared he began to have convulsions. On February 12, 1981, Earl went into heart failure during a seizure. Paramedics revived him and placed him on life support; however, doctors claimed he was brain dead and removed him from life support three days later.

Johnson's daughter Jenny Ann Wright was 11 years old and complaining of chest pains. Her doctor prescribed a rib belt and Tylenol. On February 21, 1982, paramedics found Jenny Ann face down on Johnson's bed. Foam was coming from Jenny's mouth, but the doctors were unable to revive her. An autopsy indicated that Jenny Ann had died of asphyxia.

Johnson and Bowen separated permanently, and Johnson remarried.

In December 1989, investigators determined that each child's death was preceded 7 to 10 days by marital problems between Johnson and Bowen and reopened the cases.

On July 3, 1989, the police arrested Johnson, and she confessed to suffocating two of her children. After confrontations with Bowen, Johnson would kill her children by rolling her 250-pound body on them as they slept. She wanted to punish her husband. Johnson assured she did not kill her two youngest children.

In April 1990, Johnson had rejected her confession by the beginning of her trial.

On May 5, 1990, the judge convicted of first-degree murder for the smothering deaths of three of Johnson's four children and sentenced her to death.

OUTCOME

She is in Pulaski State Prison now because the authorities later commuted the sentence to life on appeal.

GENENE JONES

◊ **Date of birth:** July 13, 1950
◊ **Motive:** Pushing herself into the role of a hero
◊ **Number of victims:** Two confirmed; possibly over 60
◊ **Date of murders:** 1977 – 1982
◊ **Date of arrest:** November 21, 1982
◊ **Murder method:** Poisoning (digoxin, heparin, and succinylcholine)
◊ **Known victims:** Infants and children
◊ **Crime location:** San Antonio, Texas, United States
◊ **Status:** On February 15, 1984, sentenced to 99 years in prison. On October 24, 1984, sentenced to a concurrent term of 60 years in prison.

BACKGROUND

A nightclub owner and his wife adopted Genene Jones. In June 1968, Jones married her high school sweetheart, James H. DeLany Jr. In 1972 the couple had a son, Richard Michael.

In 1974 they divorced, but in 1977 the DeLanys had a brief reconciliation which resulted in the birth of their second child, 6-year-old Heather.

Before attending nursing school, Genene worked as a beautician. Jones entered nursing school in 1977 in San Antonio and went to work at a local hospital. Eight months later, she resigned because of a conflict with a doctor.

After another brief stint in another hospital, she got a job on October 30, 1978, in the pediatric intensive care unit.

The co-workers respected Genene and considered her devoted to the job of nursing sick babies.

In 1982, Dr. Kathleen Holland opened a pediatric clinic in Kerrville, Texas. She employed a licensed vocational nurse named Genene Jones, who had recently resigned from the Bexar County Medical Center Hospital. Seven children had seizures over the next two months.

MURDERS

Between May and December 1981, babies admitted to the intensive care unit had begun dying at an alarming rate at the Pediatric Department of the Bexar County Hospital. The department had witnessed the loss of twenty infants through runaway bleeding or heart failure. In most cases, death had occurred while the babies were in the care of a licensed vocational nurse named Genene Jones.

Experts from hospitals held a series of internal inquiries and investigated the deaths. They interviewed members of Bexar's staff and were surprised when one of Genene's colleagues accused her of the infants' murders. The panel failed to reach a firm conclusion beyond the suggestion that the hospital fire Jones and the co-worker who had accused her of murdering babies.

Jones gained her next appointment at the Kerrville Hospital, where within months of her starting work, some children began suffering breathing problems. They all recovered, and nobody paid special attention to the incident, and Genene Jones did not come under suspicion; however, when parents brought fifteen-month-old Chelsea McClellan to the hospital for regular immunization against mumps and measles, it was Genene who gave the child her first shot, which led to an immediate seizure.

On the way to San Antonio for emergency treatment, Chelsea McClellan suffered a heart attack and died.

ARREST AND TRIAL

The healthcare authorities had become worried about the deaths at both hospitals. Genene Jones was fired pending a grand jury investigation. News reports had begun to describe forty-two baby deaths under inquiry. The jury finally returned indictments against Jones. She was convicted of murder following the discovery of succinylcholine in the McClellan baby's body.

During January and February 1985, Genene Jones was found guilty on a charge of murdering Chelsea McClellan and sentenced to ninety-nine years. The authorities put her on trial for a second time and charged her with administering an overdose of the blood-thinning drug heparin to another child, Rolando Santos. This time Jones was handed down a concurrent term of sixty years. There is general agreement that Genene took pleasure in creating life and death dramas in which she could play an influential role.

OUTCOME

As of May 2016, Jones had been scheduled for mandatory release in 2018 due to a Texas law meant to prevent prison overcrowding. To avoid this, she was indicted on May 25, 2017, for the murder of 11-month-old Joshua Sawyer. Due to the mandatory early-release law, including Jones' original convictions, she would have been released upon completion of a third of the sentence. The new indictments were filed to avoid her release.

SANTE KIMES

◊ **Date of birth:** July 24, 1934
◊ **Motive:** Financial
◊ **Number of victims:** 2
◊ **Date of murders:** 1996 – 1998
◊ **Date of arrest:** July 1998
◊ **Murder method:**
◊ **Known victims:** Syed Bilal Ahmed; David Kazdin; Irene Silverman, 82
◊ **Crime location:** The Bahamas, California, New York, United States
◊ **Status:** On June 27, 2000, sentenced to 125 years in prison in New York. In 2004 sentenced to life in prison in California

BACKGROUND

Sante Kimes was born Sandra Louise Singhrs in Oklahoma City to Mary Van Horn and Mahendra Prama Singh from East India. Sante gave many different stories about her origins, which is why her estranged son, Kent Walker, says her birth certificate might be forged.

Kent Walker wrote a book Son of a Grifter in which he reported a statement by an old friend of his mother that she was born in a reputable family who could not cope with their daughter's wild tricks. Sante Kimes has declared that her father was a laborer and her mother was a prostitute who migrated from Oklahoma.

She graduated high school in Carson City, Nevada in 1952 and soon married a high school boyfriend. Three months later, their marriage ended. Sante reunited with another sweetheart from high school, Edward Walker, in 1956. Their relationship produced one son named Kent. The couple had troubles. In 1961, Sante Kimes ended her marriage to Walker after a shoplifting conviction. She met Kenneth Kimes in 1971. Their marriage produced one son, Kenneth Kimes Jr., who was born in 1975.

According to her son's book Son of a Grifter, Sante was a robber, a forger, and an arsonist.

She often offered young, homeless illegal immigrants housing and employment, then kept them as prisoners by threatening to report them to the authorities if they did not obey her orders. Consequently, she and her second husband, alcoholic motel magnate Kenneth Kimes, spent years wasting his fortune on attorneys' fees, defending themselves against charges of slavery. In August 1985, Kimes was arrested and sentenced to five years in prison for breaking federal anti-slavery laws. Sante took a plea bargain and agreed to complete an alcohol treatment program. Kenneth Sr. and their son Kenny lived a somewhat normal life until Sante returned from prison in 1989. Ken Sr. died in 1994.

MURDERS

David Kazdin had permitted Kimes to use his name on the deed of a home in Las Vegas that was occupied by Sante Kimes and Kenneth Sr. in the 1970s. In a few years, Sante Kimes persuaded a notary to forge David's signature on an application for a loan, with the cottage as a pledge. When Kazdin revealed the falsification and threatened to expose Kimes, she ordered him killed. Ken Jr. shot Kazdin in the back of the head. According to another accomplice's later statements, all three participated in the elimination of the evidence. In March 1998, Kazdin's body was found in a dumpster near the Los Angeles airport.

In June 1998, Kimes with her son Kenneth came up with a plan that she would pretend to be their landlady, 82-year-old Irene Silverman, and then appropriate ownership of her expensive Manhattan residence. The search for Silverman went as far as Mount Olive in New Jersey. Even though Silverman's body was not found, in 2000, the authorities convicted both mother and son of murder. In the process of the trial for the Kazdin murder, Kenneth Jr. admitted that after Sante had used a stun

gun on Ms. Silverman, he smothered her, put her body in a bag and disposed of it in Hoboken, New Jersey.

Ken Jr. also confessed to killing a third man, banker Sayed Bilal Ahmed, in 1996, at his mother's behest in The Bahamas. Kenneth witnessed that the two acted together to drug Ahmed, drown him in a bathtub, and dump his body offshore, but the police filed no charges in that case.

ARREST AND TRIAL

Although the Kazdin murder happened first, the Kimeses were tried first for the murder. Evidence found in their car helped establish the case for judging them for Kazdin's killing as well.

Kenneth Kimes was extradited from New York City to Los Angeles to stand trial for the murder of David Kazdin in March 2001. In June 2001, Sante Kimes was extradited to Los Angeles too. During the trial in June 2004, Kenneth changed his plea from "not guilty" to "guilty" facing the death penalty. Sante Kimes again denied the murders and accused prosecutors and police of various kinds of misconduct. The sentencing judge ordered her to be silent and in the Kazdin case called Sante Kimes "one of the evilest individuals" she had met in her time as a judge.

OUTCOME

Sante Kimes was serving her life sentence plus 125 years at the Bedford Hills Correctional Facility for Women in New York. The Californian judge sentenced Kimes and Kenneth Jr. to life imprisonment for the murder of David Kazdin. Kenneth Kimes is still imprisoned at the Richard J. Donovan Correctional Facility in California.

On May 19, 2014, Sante Kimes died of natural causes.

SHARON KINNE

- ◊ **Date of birth:** November 30, 1939
- ◊ **Nicknames:** La Pistolera
- ◊ **Motive:** A life insurance policy. She began to derive pleasure from killing
- ◊ **Number of victims:** 3
- ◊ **Date of murders:** 1960 – 1964
- ◊ **Date of arrest:** September 18, 1964
- ◊ **Murder method:** Shooting
- ◊ **Known victims:** Her husband, James Kinne, 25; wife of Kinne's boyfriend, Patricia Jones, 23; Francisco Paredes Ordoñez
- ◊ **Crime location:** Missouri, United States; Mexico City, Mexico
- ◊ **Status:** On December 7, 1969, she escaped from the Mexican prison. Despite a huge search, nobody knows her whereabouts.

BACKGROUND

On November 30, 1939, Sharon Elizabeth Hall was born in Independence, Missouri. Her parents, Doris and Eugene Hall, moved to Washington when she was in junior high school. The family returned to Missouri when Sharon was fifteen.

Sharon was sixteen when she met twenty-two-year-old college student James Kinne at a church function in the summer of 1956. The couple dated constantly until Kinne returned to Brigham Young University in the fall. Sharon soon sent a letter to Kinne at school writing that she was pregnant by him.

James left college and came back to Independence. On October 18, 1956, he married Sharon. Their marriage license identified Sharon as being eighteen and a widow. The next year, the couple had a more formal wedding in the Salt Lake Temple.

Together they went back to Provo, Utah. Kinne had been attending college there, but at the end of the fall, Kinne again stopped studying. He and his wife returned to Independence, and both took jobs. Sharon was a babysitter and tended shops; James was an electrical engineer at Bendix Aviation. Sharon soon became pregnant and gave birth to a girl Danna in the fall of 1957.

Sharon expected excellent things out of life, but on Kinne's salary, they lived in a rented home, and then in a ranch-style house they had built in Independence. She filled her days with shopping and with other men while Kinne worked the night shift at Bendix. Soon the couple had a second child, Troy, and Sharon was carrying on an affair with her friend from high school days, John Boldizs.

By early 1960, James Kinne was considering divorce because of his wife's spendthrift habits and because he strongly suspected she was unfaithful. On March 18, 1960, he spoke to his parents about the possibility of divorce, but the elder Kinnes convinced James to stay in the marriage. According to John Boldizs, Sharon once offered him $1,000 to kill her husband or find someone who would.

MURDERS

On the evening of March 19, Sharon Kinne heard a gunshot from the bedroom where her husband was sleeping. When Sharon entered the room, she found their two-and-a-half-year-old daughter on the bed near her father. Danna was holding one of her father's guns, a .22 caliber pistol. James had a gunshot wound in the back of his head. Sharon called the police, but James Kinne was dead by the time the ambulance carrying him arrived at the hospital.

Police could not discover fingerprints from the well-oiled grip of the pistol, and Danna or Sharon Kinne did not pass a paraffin test for gunshot residue. Family members and neighbors told police that James had allowed Danna to play with his guns, so the investigators ruled the case an accidental homicide.

The pistol that killed James Kinne was taken into police custody and never returned to the widow, despite her efforts to reclaim it.

Sharon buried her husband and collected on his life insurance policies, valued at about $29,000.

Patricia Jones was born Patricia Clements; after graduating from a local high school she married Walter T. Jones, Jr. who enlisted in the Marine Corps shortly after their marriage. After his discharge from the military, Walter sold automobiles.

Walter Jones had a wandering eye. In April, he met Sharon when she bought a Ford Thunderbird from his dealership; the two began an affair shortly after that. Kinne wanted to marry him, but Jones was uninterested in leaving his wife. The relationship was on the rocks after Sharon told Walter that she was pregnant. Jones was the father of the baby. Walter ended the affair, instead of responding with what Kinne expected to be an agreement to divorce his wife.

On May 26, Kinne called Patricia Jones and told her that her husband was having an affair with Sharon's sister. Kinne met with Patricia Jones that evening to discuss the matter.

Patricia Jones never returned to her house. Walter Jones filed a missing person report with police the next day. He spoke to friends of Patricia's who worked with her. The friends described to Jones the woman who was waiting for Jones in a car at the shop.

Suspicious, Walter Jones called Kinne and asked if she had met his wife. Kinne replied that she had seen Patricia that day to tell her about their affair.

Kinne called John Boldizs and asked him to help her search for Patricia Jones. Within several hours of Kinne's conversation with Walter Jones, she and Boldizs found the body of a woman one mile outside of Independence.

Walter Jones identified the body as the missing Patricia Jones. Sharon had hit Walter's wife with four shots from a .22 caliber pistol.

She was buried on May 31.

ARREST AND TRIAL

The police officers immediately began questioning Sharon Kinne, James Boldizs, and Walter Jones. On May 28, investigators interviewed all three. Boldizs and Jones gave written statements acknowledging to have been dating Sharon Kinne. Both agreed to lie detector tests. Sharon Kinne spoke to police but refused to sign a written statement or take a lie detector test.

While police officers questioned potential suspects, other investigators focused on the murder weapon.

Boy Scouts eventually found a .22 caliber rifle slug buried in the ground where Kinne and Boldizs had found Jones's body.

The gun that had killed Kinne's husband was still in the possession of the sheriff's office, and the police ruled out the .22 caliber pistol that had killed Kinne's husband as the murder weapon in Jones's death. However, one man who worked with Kinne confessed to having purchased a new .22 caliber pistol at her request in May.

On May 31, Kinne was arrested at her home for murder, and the Jackson County Sheriff requested that prosecutors consider the second charge of manslaughter for the death of James Kinne.

On July 11, the Kansas City Court of Appeals struck down the denial of bail on circumstantial evidence. On July 18, they freed Kinne on $24,000 bond.

On January 16, 1961, Kinne gave birth to a daughter, Marla Christine.

Sharon Kinne was tried separately for the murders of Patricia Jones and James Kinne.

Kinne, still free on bond, traveled to Mexico with her lover, Francis Samuel Puglise in September 1964. The pair later stated that they had come to Mexico to get married. After crossing the border, they registered at a local hotel as husband and wife. Kinne bought a pistol although the couple brought one or two with them from the United States.

On September 18, 1964, Kinne left the hotel without Pugliese to get medicine she required. She met Francisco Parades Ordoñez at a bar and accompanied him back to his room in Hotel La Vada.

In his room, he began to make sexual advances toward her, and she fired her gun to protect herself. Having heard gunfire, hotel employee Enrique Martinez Rueda entered the room. Kinne shot and hit Rueda in the shoulder. Wounded, Rueda locked Kinne inside and called the police.

Rejecting Kinne's story, police assumed that she had gone out intending robbery, and had chosen Ordoñez as a victim. After he refused to give her his money, police theorized Kinne had shot him.

Authorities proved through ballistics that the gun found in the couple's room was the same gun that killed Patricia Jones in 1960, but because the court had already acquitted Kinne of that crime, they could not charge her again based

on the new evidence.

In the summer of 1965, both Kinne and Pugliese were tried. Kinne was sentenced to a ten-year prison term for the crimes.

Sharon Kinne was not present for a 5 p.m. roll-call at the Ixtapalapan prison on December 7, 1969. Her absence was not reported until she did not show up at a second roll-call later that evening. Mexico City police did not know about her disappearance until 2 a.m. the following morning. The authorities arranged a search focusing on the northern Mexican states. The initial police assumption was that Kinne had corrupted guards, but further questioning of administration and correctional officers showed that supervision at the prison was weak.

A modern theory about Kinne's escape suggests that Francisco Parades Ordoñez's family had helped her escape and then killed her.

Despite promising to keep the case open and their search running until Kinne was back in prison, in December 1969, the authorities admitted that they had run out of investigative leads.

OUTCOME

Kinne remains at large more than forty years after her escape. Her whereabouts and fate are unknown.

TILLIE KLIMEK

◊ **Date of birth:** 1876
◊ **Other names:** Ottilie Gburek
◊ **Motive:** When she was scheduling her victims' deaths, she pretended to have prophetic dreams, accurately predicting the dates.
◊ **Number of victims:** 5 – 7
◊ **Date of murders:** 1914 – 1921
◊ **Date of arrest:** 1921
◊ **Murder method:** Poisoning (arsenic)
◊ **Known victims:** Her third known husband, Frank Kupzsyk
◊ **Crime location:** Illinois, United States
◊ **Status:** On November 20, 1936, died in prison

BACKGROUND

Tillie Klimek was born Otillie Gburek in Poland, and with her parents, she came to the United States as an infant. She married her original husband John Mitkiewicz, c. 1890, but he died after a short illness in 1914. The death certificate listed heart trouble as the cause of death. Klimek quickly remarried Joseph Ruskowski, who lived nearby. He also died in short order, as did a boyfriend who had "jilted" her.

MURDERS

The crime for which she was tried was the murder of her third husband, Frank Kupzsyk. He had taken ill in their apartment where Tillie had lived with her previous boyfriend, Meyers. Tillie began to tell neighbors that Frank "would soon die.' She mocked Frank, greeting him in the morning by saying, "You'll die soon." She even knitted her funeral hat as she sat at his bedside.

In 1921, after Frank's death, she married Joseph Klimek. Soon he became ill, and doctors suspected arsenic poisoning. They conducted tests which confirmed it and authorities arrested Tillie.

The authorities permitted exhuming the bodies of her other husbands, which contained lethal doses of arsenic, though the soil around the bodies was clean. Klimek had told police officers that she had told her cousin, Nellie that she was tired of her husband, Frank. Nellie suggested divorce. Tillie said that she would get rid of him and declared that Nellie had provided her with a goodly portion of a poison called "Rough on Rats." Police also arrested Nellie.

ARREST AND TRIAL

After the arrest, it turned out that several neighbors and relatives of both women had died. Tillie had quarreled with two neighbors, and they became ill after she gave them candies. Several of the two women's cousins and relatives were found to have become sick shortly after eating at Tillie's house. In all, the list stretched to twenty-two victims, fourteen of whom had died. Joseph Klimek survived, though he had spent a lot of time in the hospital.

In March of 1923, the jury found Tillie guilty of the murder of her third known husband, Frank Kupzsyk, and the judge sentenced her to life in prison.

OUTCOME

On November 20, 1936, Tillie died in prison.

THERESA KNORR

- ◊ **Date of birth:** March 14, 1946
- ◊ **Number of victims:** 2 – 3
- ◊ **Date of murders:** 1984 – 1985
- ◊ **Date of arrest:** November 11, 1993
- ◊ **Murder method:** Parricide, torture (dousing with gasoline and setting afire; dehydration and starvation)
- ◊ **Known victims:** Her daughters: Suesan Marlene Knorr, 17, Sheila Gail Sanders, 20
- ◊ **Crime location:** Placer County, Sacramento County, California, United States
- ◊ **Status:** On October 17, 1995, sentenced to two consecutive life terms

BACKGROUND

Theresa Knorr was born Theresa Jimmie Francine Cross in Sacramento, California. Her parents were Jim Cross and Swannie Gay. Theresa was the youngest child in the family and very devoted to her mother. She went into a depression when her mother died in 1961. At the age of 16, Cross married Clifford Clyde Sanders. They had a son, Howard, but quarreled and fought from time to time. In 1964 she shot her husband dead. Theresa was tried, and the jury found her not guilty. She was pregnant at the time, and in 1965 she gave birth to her second child, Sheila.

In 1966, being seven months pregnant, she married Robert Knorr. They had a child Suesan born in September 1966. One year later they had a son William.

Robert was her fifth, born in 1968.

Knorr was verbally, psychologically, and physically abusive towards her children, and her alcoholism and abusive behavior increased after her fourth divorce. She also became overweight and quick-tempered. Knorr disconnected the home phone and would not allow anyone to visit her house. Her neighbors claimed that the apartment was dirty and smelly. Neighbors also noticed that the children seemed fearful, nervous, and high-strung.

Knorr abused and tortured her children, force-feeding them, beating them, throwing knives at them and burning them with cigarettes. In one case, she held a pistol to her daughter Terry's head and threatened to kill her.

Knorr also believed that her husband, Chet Harris, had turned Suesan into a witch, so Knorr abused her more than the other children. After one harsh beating, Suesan escaped the home. The police picked her up and placed her in a psychiatric hospital. Knorr denied her daughter's abuse claims and told the hospital staff that Suesan had mental problems. Authorities did not investigate the case further and released Suesan back into her mother's "care." Knorr punished Suesan for fleeing by beating her while wearing a pair of leather gloves. She also made her other children beat their sister. Knorr handcuffed Suesan to her bed; refused to let her leave the house, and ordered her to drop out of school. She also pulled her other children out of school, and most of them never advanced past the eighth grade.

She trained her sons to beat her daughters to discipline them. She burned her oldest daughter Suesan alive; she then killed her second daughter, Sheila, by starvation.

MURDERS

In 1983 in a heated argument with her daughter, Knorr grabbed a 22-caliber pistol and shot Suesan in the chest. She survived, but the bullet became lodged in her back. Without professional treatment, Suesan recovered from her wounds.

In 1984, Suesan decided to move out. Knorr agreed under the condition that she would remove the bullet from Suesan's back. The anesthetic was liquor. Knorr ordered her son Robert to remove

the bullet with a box cutter. Suesan's skin turned yellow from infection, and she lay dying on the floor. Knorr told her other children that Suesan's ailment was a result of possession by Satan and that the only way to purge the devil was with fire. She forced Robert and Bill into helping her dispose of Suesan. They drove her to the Sierra Nevada Mountains, laid her down, poured gasoline on her, and burned her alive.

In 1985, Sheila also died at the hands of her mother. According to Terry, Knorr forced Sheila into becoming a prostitute. Knorr blamed her daughter for transmitting sexually transmitted diseases to her via a toilet seat. After that, Knorr locked Sheila in a closet where she died of starvation and dehydration. Knorr and her other children packed Sheila's body in a cardboard box and dumped it along the side of a road. She remained unidentified for years.

ARREST AND TRIAL

In 1993 Knorr and her sons were arrested. At first, she pled not guilty, but when she knew that one of her sons was going to testify against her, she pled guilty to all charges to avoid capital punishment. The judge sentenced her to two consecutive life terms.

OUTCOME

In 2027 she will be eligible for parole.

MICHELLE KNOTEK

◊ **Date of birth:** April 15, 1954
◊ **Nickname:** Crazy Shellie
◊ **Number of victims:** 2 - 3
◊ **Date of murders:** 1994 - 2003
◊ **Date of arrest:** August 8, 2003
◊ **Murder method:** Prolonged abuse
◊ **Known victims:** Kathy Loreno, 36, and Ronald Woodworth, 57
◊ **Crime location:** Washington, United States
◊ **Status:** On August 18, 2004, sentenced to 22 years in prison

MURDERS

When Kathy Loreno met Michelle Knotek, she was a hairdresser, and the two became friends. After a severe argument between Loreno and her family in 1991, Loreno moved out of their home and into the home of Michelle and David Knotek. During her stay at the Knoteks' house, Loreno suffered physical abuse.

In 1994, family members reported Loreno missing. The authorities interviewed the Knoteks who stated that Loreno escaped with a truck driver and moved to Hawaii; however, Loreno's brother hired a private investigator, who concluded that Michelle Knotek had presumably murdered her.

Michelle Knotek had a nephew, Shane Watson, born in 1975, in Tacoma. Around 1993, he moved in with the Knoteks. In 1994, shortly after Loreno's disappearance, Watson vanished too. The Knoteks claimed that Watson had fled to Alaska to work on a fishing ship.

David Knotek later declared that he had shot Watson with a .22 caliber rifle.

Investigators claimed that David Knotek killed Watson because Michelle saw that Watson took pictures documenting the abuse of Loreno. David Knotek also stated that he burned the bodies of Shane Watson and Kathy Loreno and scattered their ashes at the beach.

A local man, Ronald Woodworth, went to live with the Knoteks around 2001. Woodworth was also subject to brutal physical abuse. Witnesses said they had seen Woodworth being ordered to do chores in the open air wearing only his underwear. He was also forced to jump from the second level roof onto a gritty surface with bare feet causing severe lacerations and broken bones.

They also asserted that Knotek would burn his injured feet with pure bleach and boiling water. In 2003 Woodworth went missing. David Knotek later confessed to burying the body on their property. An autopsy by the King County medical examiner proved that Woodworth was murdered.

ARREST AND TRIAL

The Pacific County Deputy Prosecutor set out that Michelle Knotek demonstrated "excess indifferent attitude to human life." The judge charged Michelle with first-degree murder of Kathy Loreno and Ronald Woodworth.

In 2004 Michelle Knotek pleaded guilty and entered an Alford plea, in which she confirmed the prosecutor's case against her. The judge Mark McCauley sentenced her to 22 years in prison.

OUTCOME

The daughters do not communicate with their mother, because they are afraid any contact with her can endanger them and their families.

SHEILA LABARRE

- ◊ **Date of birth:** 4 July 1958
- ◊ **Nicknames:** Sheila the Peeler; Firecracker
- ◊ **Motive:** Obsession with pedophiles
- ◊ **Number of victims:** 2 - 4
- ◊ **Date of murders:** 2004 - 2006
- ◊ **Date of arrest:** April 2, 2006
- ◊ **Murder method:** Beating
- ◊ **Known victims:** Michael Deloge, 38; Kenneth Countie, 24
- ◊ **Crime location:** New Hampshire, United States
- ◊ **Status:** On June 20, 2008, sentenced to two life sentences with no possibility of parole

BACKGROUND

Born in 1958, Sheila LaBarre, nee Bailey, grew up in Fort Payne, Alabama. She insists that she had been sexually abused when she was a child, mainly at her father's hands.

On New Year's Eve 1981, Bailey married John Baxter. Sheila was 23, and her husband was 19. After only six weeks of marriage, Baxter discovered that Bailey had been locking his little girl in a small room when he was working. After Valentine's Day, he divorced her.

Sheila moved to Chattanooga with her next husband, Ronnie Jennings. It wasn't a happy marriage.

Ronnie said Sheila was an unbalanced woman. After a suicide attempt, she was placed in a psych ward during their unhappy four-year marriage. Bailey's wild mood swings often turned cruel.

Ronnie's mom, Cathryn Jennings, said her son once lay awake all night afraid his wife could kill him with scissors.

Wilfred J. LaBarre placed a personal ad. Sheila Bailey Jennings answered it and moved to Epping, New Hampshire in 1987. LaBarre was a respected chiropractor. A widower, he was quite well off having a million-dollar horse farm in Epping.

The man did not want to marry Sheila, but she took his name. Sheila also became his office manager, and after their "romance" petered out, she lived in an apartment above his office in Hampton.

In 1995, Sheila LaBarre married a native of Jamaica, Wayne Ennis. Again, it wasn't a happy marriage. Sheila wrote complaints to Hampton District Court, in which she stated that Ennis attempted to force her car off the road, then struck her in the head and kicked her. In 1996 she divorced him but stayed in touch.

Sheila LaBarre also stayed in touch with Bill LaBarre and chased the man with a gun. She also asked her ex Wayne Ennis to kill Bill so that she could take over his farm. That was according to Laura Melisi who went to the court requesting a restraining order to keep Sheila away from her dad. The court granted a restraining order for a year.

MURDERS

Kenny Countie

In 2006 a twenty-year-old Kenny Countie met LaBarre via a personal ad. He moved in with her shortly after their meeting. Countie had a low IQ and "childlike" trust. LaBarre recorded him vomiting and she accused him of being a pedophile. She stabbed him to death and then burned the body. The police identified Kenny's DNA from his army records.

His mother subsequently accused the Epping Police Department of negligence. Before his death, people had seen him in a wheelchair in a Walmart store, bruised and burned. In 2010, the authorities rejected her lawsuit against the two police officers who had seen him in the store.

Michael Deloge

Michael was LaBarre's boyfriend. The pair lived at her farm. In 2005 people saw him for the last time. In 2008 the police found his bones and his birth certificate at the farm. It is unknown how he died. Deloge's mother informed the police that she was worried LaBarre was trying to kill him.

ARREST AND TRIAL

On April 1, 2006, the police issued an arrest warrant for Shelia LaBarre, and charged with first-degree murder. On April 2, the authorities arrested her, and the police conducted a three-week search of her farm, which led to the discovery of three human toes which forensic analysis determined did not belong to either Kenny Countie or Michael Deloge.

The jury came to LaBarre's farm and visited the Walmart where people had seen her with Countie. LaBarre, wearing a stun belt, attended too. She pleaded not guilty to murdering Countie and Deloge. Her defense attorney told she looked like a "deeply sick individual."

In May 2008, psychiatrists diagnosed LaBarre with schizoaffective disorder and delusional disorder.

LaBarre's ex-husband Wayne Ennis stated that she had asked him to kill Wilfred.

The jury rejected LaBarre's plea of not guilty because of insanity. In 2008, they found LaBarre guilty, and the judge sentenced her to life in prison without parole.

OUTCOME

Her appeal in 2010 was rejected. LaBarre is serving her sentence at Homestead Correctional Institution, in Florida City, Florida.

DELPHINE LALAURIE

- ◊ **Date of birth:** 19 March 1787
- ◊ **Other names:** Marie Delphine LaLaurie, Marie Delphine Macarty LaLaurie, Delphine Maccarthy LaLaurie, Madame LaLaurie
- ◊ **Number of victims:** Several
- ◊ **Date of murders:** 1831 – 1834
- ◊ **Date of arrest:** 1834
- ◊ **Murder method:** Starvation, Torture
- ◊ **Known victims:** Blacks, slaves
- ◊ **Crime location:** New Orleans, Louisiana, United States
- ◊ **Status:** Fled before she could be brought to justice and was never caught. On December 7, 1842, she died in Paris.

BACKGROUND

Delphine Macarty was born around 1775, one of five children. Around 1730, her grandfather, Barthelmy Macarty, brought the family to New Orleans from Ireland. Her father was Barthelmy Louis Macarty. Her mother was Marie Jeanne Lovable whose marriage to Barthelmy Louis Macarty was her second. Both were prominent members of the New Orleans white Créole community.

On June 11, 1800, Delphine Macarty married Don Ramon de Lopez y Angullo, a Caballero de la Royal de Carlos at the Saint Louis Cathedral in New Orleans. By 1804, Don Ramon had risen to the position of consul general for Spain in Louisiana. Also, in 1804, Delphine and Don Ramon traveled to Spain. Accounts of the trip differ. In 1921 Grace King wrote that the trip was Don Ramon's "military punishment," and that Delphine met the Queen, who was impressed by Delphine's beauty.

Stanley Arthur's 1936 report stated that on March 26, 1804, Don Ramon was recalled to the court of Spain "to take his place at court as befitting his new position," but that Ramon never arrived in Spain because he died in Havana en route to Madrid.

During the trip, Delphine gave birth to a daughter, named Marie Borgia Delphine Lopez y Angulla de la Candelaria. Delphine and her daughter, Borquita, returned to New Orleans afterward.

Delphine married a prominent banker, merchant, lawyer, and legislator, Jean Blanque, in June 1808. The same year Blanque purchased a house at 409 Royal Street in New Orleans for the family.

Delphine had four more children named Marie Louise Pauline, Louise Marie Laure, Marie Louise Jeanne, and Jeanne Pierre Paulin Blanque.

In 1816, Blanque died. On June 25, 1825, Delphine married a physician Leonard Louis Nicolas LaLaurie, who was much younger than she. She bought property at 1140 Royal Street in 1831, and by 1832 she had built a three-story mansion there, complete with attached slave quarters. She lived there with her husband and two of her daughters and maintained a central position in the social circles of New Orleans.

MURDERS

The LaLauries maintained several black slaves. Data of Delphine LaLaurie's treatments of her slaves between 1831 and 1834 is different. In 1838, Harriet Martineau, writing tales told by New Orleans residents during her 1836 visit, claimed LaLaurie's slaves were seen to be emaciated and miserable. However, in public, LaLaurie was generally polite to black people and caring of her slaves' health. In 1819 LaLaurie emancipated one of her slaves, Jean Louis. In 1832 she freed another one, Devince. Nevertheless, a local lawyer visited Royal Street to remind LaLaurie of the laws relevant to the upkeep of slaves. During the visit, the lawyer found no confirmation of the cruel treatment of slaves by LaLaurie.

Martineau also claimed that, after the visit of the lawyer, one of the neighbors observed one of the LaLaurie's slaves, a twelve-year-old girl, fall to her death from the roof while trying to avoid punishment from Delphine LaLaurie. The LaLauries buried the body on the mansion grounds. This occurrence led to an investigation, in which the authorities found the LaLauries guilty of mistreatment and forced them to forfeit nine slaves. The LaLauries repurchased these slaves and returned them to the residences. Martineau reported stories that LaLaurie chained her cook to the kitchen stove and beat her daughters when they attempted to feed starving slaves.

A fire started in the kitchen in LaLaurie's residence on April 10, 1834. When fire marshals and the police got there, they found a seventy-year-old cook chained to the stove by her ankle. The cook confessed that she had set the fire as a suicide attempt for fear of her punishment. She explained: "Anyone who had been taken to the uppermost room, never came back." On April 11, 1834, the New Orleans Bee reported that bystanders attempted to enter the slave quarters to ensure that firefighters had evacuated everyone. The LaLauries refused to give them the keys, and the bystanders broke down the doors to the slave quarters. They found "seven slaves, more or less mutilated and suspended by the neck, with their limbs stretched from one extremity to the other." They claimed to have been imprisoned there for several months.

Judge Jean-Francois Canonge was among those who entered the premises. He found in the LaLaurie mansion, among others, a "negro girl in an iron collar" and "an old negro woman with a very deep wound on her head." Canonge questioned Madame LaLaurie's husband about the slaves and was told that "he had better stay at home rather than come to others' houses to dictate laws."

Soon the discovery of the tortured slaves became widely known, and a crowd of locals attacked the residence and "demolished and destroyed everything upon which they could lay their hands." A sheriff and his officers were required to disperse the mob and, by the time the crowd left, the property had major damage, with "scarcely anything remaining but the walls."

The authorities put the tortured slaves in jail, where everyone could view them publicly.

The Pittsfield Sun, citing the New Orleans Advertiser, claimed that two of the slaves had died since the rescue, and added: "We understand that in digging up the yard, bodies have been disinterred, and the condemned well having been uncovered, others, particularly that of a child, were found."

ARREST AND TRIAL

After the 1834 fire, LaLaurie's life is not well documented. In 1838, Martineau wrote that LaLaurie fled New Orleans during the crowd violence that followed the fire. She took a coach to the waterfront and traveled by schooner to Mobile, Alabama and then on to Paris. In 1836, Martineau personally visited the Royal Street mansion. It was still empty and badly damaged, with "gaping windows and empty walls."

OUTCOME

It is not clear how Delphine LaLaurie died. George Washington Cable recounted in 1888 an unsubstantiated story that she had died in France in a boar-hunting accident. Whatever the truth, Eugene Backes in the late 1930s, who served as sexton to St. Louis Cemetery #1, discovered a cracked copper plate in Alley 4 of the cemetery. English translation of the inscription on the plate reads: "Madame LaLaurie, born Marie Delphine Macarty, died in Paris, on December 7, 1842, at the age of 62."

RHONDA BELLE MARTIN

- ◊ **Date of birth:** 1907
- ◊ **Nickname:** Black Widow
- ◊ **Motive:** To collect insurance money
- ◊ **Number of victims:** 6
- ◊ **Date of murders:** 1937 – 1951
- ◊ **Date of arrest:** March 1956
- ◊ **Murder method:** Poisoning (arsenic)
- ◊ **Known victims:** Her daughter Emogene Garrett, 3; her second husband George Garrett; her daughter Anna Carolyn Garrett, 6; her daughter Ellyn Elizabeth Garrett, 11; Mrs. Mary Frances Gibbon (her mother); her fourth husband Claude Carroll Martin, 51.
- ◊ **Crime location:** Montgomery, Alabama, United States
- ◊ **Status:** On October 11, 1957, executed by electrocution in Alabama.

MURDERS, ARREST AND TRIAL, OUTCOME

A waitress, Rhonda Belle Martin, lived in Montgomery, Alabama. Rhonda was a daughter of James Robert Thomley and Mary Frances Gipson. When she was 12, her father deserted her family. Martin poisoned her former son-in-law, who was her fifth husband. He survived but remained paraplegic.

His illness led the police to investigate the strange deaths surrounding Rhonda. In March 1956 Martin confessed to poisoning her two husbands, three of her children and her mother. She rejected killing her two other children.

The prosecution stated that her motive was collecting insurance money, but she never admitted that.

In 1951, the judge convicted her of murdering 51-year-old Claude Martin by covertly feeding him rat poison. She was sentenced to die in the electric chair.

Eight days before death she was asked in an interview if she was ready to die: "Well, you've never seen anybody ready to sit down in the electric chair. But if that is what it has got to be, that is what it will be."

Rhonda wanted her sentence changed to life imprisonment. She had made herself a beautiful black and white dress to go to her hearing. Despite the effort, on October 11, 1957, Rhonda Belle Martin, wearing her new dress and a wedding ring, walked toward the death chamber.

She ate a hamburger, mashed potatoes, cinnamon rolls, and coffee as her last meal.

Several minutes after midnight, the officers strapped her into the chair and asked if she had anything to say. She shook her head silently. The switch was thrown; Rhonda Belle stiffened while the electricity entered her body. Then she was pronounced dead.

KIMBERLY MCCARTHY

- ◊ **Date of birth:** May 11, 1961
- ◊ **Motive:** Robbery, crack addict
- ◊ **Number of victims:** 1 – 3
- ◊ **Date of murders:** December 1988 – July 21, 1997
- ◊ **Date of arrest:** July 22, 1997
- ◊ **Murder method:** Stabbing with knife
- ◊ **Known victims:** Maggie Harding, 81; Jettie Lucas, 85; her next-door neighbor Dorothy Booth, 71.
- ◊ **Crime location:** Lancaster, Dallas County, Texas, United States
- ◊ **Status:** On June 26, 2013, executed by lethal injection

BACKGROUND

Kimberly McCarthy was born on May 11, 1961, in Greenville, Texas. She was an occupational therapist in a nursing home. McCarthy was briefly married to Aaron Michaels, and they had a son. Being an adult, she became addicted to crack cocaine. She was convicted of forgery and had convictions for prostitution and theft of services in 1990.

MURDERS

On July 21, 1997, McCarthy called her neighbor, former college psychology professor Dorothy Booth, saying that she would come to borrow some sugar. McCarthy arrived at Booth's home and beat her with a chandelier. She then stabbed her five times with a butcher knife and cut off her finger. The motive was to steal her neighbor's diamond wedding ring, purse, and Mercedes-Benz. She pawned the diamond ring to buy drugs.

ARREST AND TRIAL

The next day the police caught McCarthy and charged her with murder. McCarthy used her neighbor's credit cards at a liquor store and kept her driver's license. Police officers recovered the murder weapon from McCarthy's home and found Booth's DNA on it.

In 1998, a Dallas County, Texas jury convicted McCarthy of murdering Booth. During the hearing, prosecutors presented blood DNA evidence alleging that McCarthy also killed two other senior women in Dallas County in December 1988, 85-year-old Jettie Lucas and 81-year-old Maggie Harding, to purchase cocaine. The authorities did not charge McCarthy with those murders. The officials sentenced McCarthy to die by lethal injection for killing Booth on November 24, 1998.

In 2002, McCarthy successfully appealed her conviction, but was later re-sentenced to death on November 1, 2002.

In July 2012, McCarthy's final federal appeal was denied. In January 2013, the United States Supreme Court rejected her attorneys' writ of certiorari. January 29, 2013 was her execution date. She was granted a stay of execution only hours before her lethal injection was scheduled to occur. Her execution was then set for April 3, 2013, but the Dallas County district attorney announced in late March that the date had been moved to June 26, 2013.

OUTCOME

On June 26, 2013, fifty-two-year-old Kimberly McCarthy was executed by lethal injection at the Huntsville Unit in Huntsville, Texas. Since the death penalty was renewed in the United States in 1976, McCarthy was the 500th convicted murderer to be executed by lethal injection in Texas.

Her last words were, "This is not a loss. This is a win. You know where I'm going. I'm going home to be with Jesus. Keep the faith. I love you all."

BLANCHE TAYLOR MOORE

- ◊ **Date of birth:** February 17, 1933
- ◊ **Nickname:** Black Widow
- ◊ **Motive:** Money
- ◊ **Number of victims:** 3 confirmed
- ◊ **Date of murders:** 1968 – 1989
- ◊ **Date of arrest:** July 18, 1989
- ◊ **Murder method:**
  Poisoning (arsenic)
- ◊ **Known victims:** Her father
  P. D. Kiser; her mother-
  in-law Isla Taylor; her first
  husband James N. Taylor; her
  boyfriend, Raymond Reid.
- ◊ **Crime location:** Alamance County,
  North Carolina, United States
- ◊ **Status:** On January 18, 1991,
  sentenced to death

BACKGROUND

Blanche Moore was born Blanche Kiser to Parker Davis Kiser, mill-worker, an ordained Baptist minister, and womanizer. Her mother was Flonnie Blanche (born Honeycutt). Her father was an alcoholic, who later forced his daughter into prostitution to pay his gambling debts. In 1966, Kiser died, and the cause was reported to be a heart attack.

MURDERS

Moore married James Napoleon Taylor, a veteran and furniture restorer in 1952. The couple had two children, one in 1953 and another in 1959.

She started working at Kroger as a cashier in 1954. By 1959, she had been promoted to head cashier. She began an affair with Raymond Reid in 1962. He was the manager of the store where Moore worked.

After Moore had begun her relationship with Reid, Taylor died. Again, the doctors reported the cause as a heart attack.

Moore and Reid began dating publicly after her husband's death in 1971. By 1985, however, they had broken up. She began to date Kevin Denton, who was the regional manager for the Triad area. That relationship also ended, and in October 1985, Moore filed a sexual harassment lawsuit against Denton and Kroger. Denton resigned, and Kroger settled the case out of court two years later for $275,000.

Before leaving Kroger, Moore had met Rev. Dwight Moore. She hid her relationship with Rev. Moore because her lawsuit against Kroger claimed that she was "completely alienated towards men and has not been able to maintain any meaningful social contacts with the opposite sex." While Moore was dating Rev. Moore, she asked him to purchase some arsenic-based ant killer for her.

In 1986, doctors diagnosed Reid with a case of shingles. In April 1986, he was hospitalized and died on October 7 of that year. Doctors indicated Guillain-Barré syndrome was the cause of death.

Shortly after Reid's death, Reverend Dwight Moore and Blanche began dating publicly. The pair planned to marry, but in 1987, doctors diagnosed Blanche Moore with breast cancer. They pushed the wedding date back to November 1988, but Moore developed a mysterious intestinal illness that required two surgeries to correct. The couple was married on 19 April 1989 and had a long honeymoon in New Jersey. Shortly after their return, Rev. Moore fell ill. Doctors determined that the cause was arsenic poisoning. They conducted some tests which showed that Rev. Moore had survived the largest dose of arsenic from which a victim had not died.

The North Carolina State Bureau of Investigation conducted exhumations on Taylor, Reid, and Moore's father. The autopsies determined increased levels of arsenic in the bodies. Doctors at Baptist Hospital had requested Raymond Reid's toxicology screen. The results showed that his body had a massive amount of arsenic. The resident caring for Reid rotated to another hospital on the day the test came back, and the new resident did not pass the results of the test up the chain of command. As a result, Reid received his fatal doses of arsenic in a hospital bed.

Blanche Moore tried to change Dwight Moore's pension, so that she would be the principal beneficiary. The SBI got suspicious of her when they found out. She also lied to the SBI about how much money she had gained from Raymond Reid's estate. During questioning, Blanche Moore mentioned that both Dwight Moore and Raymond Reid felt depressed and had probably been taking arsenic.

ARREST AND TRIAL

On July 18, 1989, the police arrested Blanche Taylor Moore and charged her with the first-degree murder of Raymond Reid.

In Dwight Moore's case, it was much more challenging to find out who was poisoning him because the doctors had recognized the signs of arsenic poisoning early on.

On October 21, 1990, the trial opened in Winston-Salem. Moore firmly disclaimed ever giving Reid food. The state, however, brought fifty-three witnesses who testified about Moore's daily visits to the hospital with food.

On November 14, the jury convicted her, and on November 17, the jury recommended the death penalty. The presiding judge sentenced Moore to die by lethal injection on January 18, 1991. Moore currently resides at the North Carolina Correctional Institution for Women. She spends her time writing poetry.

Moore has been able to postpone execution for over 20 years because of the automatic appeals in progress.

In 2010 Moore filed a motion to convert her sentence to life imprisonment based on the state's Racial Justice Act.

BOOK AND FILM

Author Jim Schutze wrote a book entitled Preacher's Girl in 1993. The book is about the murders. Later the same year, Elizabeth Montgomery starred as Moore in the film "Black Widow Murders: The Blanche Taylor Moore Story" based on the book.

JUDITH ANN ADAMS NEELLEY

- ◊ **Date of birth:** June 7, 1964
- ◊ **Nickname:** Lady Sundown
- ◊ **Motive:** Kidnapping, rape, torture murders
- ◊ **Number of victims:** 2
- ◊ **Date of murders:** 1982
- ◊ **Date of arrest:** October 9, 1982
- ◊ **Murder method:** Shooting
- ◊ **Known victims:** Lisa Ann Millican, 13; Janice Kay Chatman, 22
- ◊ **Crime location:** Alabama, Georgia, United States
- ◊ **Status:** On April 18, 1983, sentenced to death in Alabama. On January 15, 1999, commuted to life imprisonment.

BACKGROUND

Judith Adams was born in Murfreesboro, Tennessee on June 7, 1964. When she was nine, her father, an alcoholic, died. She began her life of crime after meeting Alvin Neelley. She committed armed robbery across the country, and the police later caught her. While incarcerated at Rome's Youth Development Center, she gave birth to twins.

MURDERS

Ken Dooley was a Youth Development Center employee. Her home was shot through four times on September 11, 1982. Linda Adair was Dooley's fellow employee. The following day, somebody firebombed her home with a Molotov cocktail. Following the attacks, a female made phone calls to the victims. She claimed to have been sexually abused at the Youth Development Center, but neither victim could identify her voice.

On September 25, 1982, a 13-year-old girl, Lisa Ann Millican, from Georgia was abducted by Alvin and Judith Neelley from the Riverbend Mall. The Neelleys took her to a Murfreesboro, Tennessee motel where they held her captive. During her captivity, both Neelleys molested Lisa, and Judith injected her with Drano. On the 28th, Judith shot Lisa in the head, and the couple threw the body in the Little River Canyon in Fort Payne, Alabama. Judith even reported to the police about Lisa's body.

John Hancock and Janice Chatman were a young engaged couple living in Rome, Georgia. Judith Neelley took them away on October 4, 1982. The Neelleys shot John Hancock and brought Janice Chatman back to their motel room, where they tortured and murdered her. John Hancock did not die however, and was able to point to Alvin and Judith Neelley as his assailants.

ARREST AND TRIAL

On October 9, 1982, the police arrested Judith Neelley and took Alvin into custody a few days later. The authorities deduced Judith was the perpetrator in the YDC employee attacks.

Alvin Neelley pled guilty to murder in Georgia to avoid the death penalty.

On March 7, 1983, Judith Neelley's trial began. Behind bars, she gave birth to a third child. After a six-week trial, the authorities convicted Judith of the torture murder of Lisa Ann Millican. Judge Randall Cole sentenced the 18-year-old mother of three to death in Alabama's electric chair despite a jury's recommendation to sentence her to life in prison.

Judith pled guilty to Janice Chatman's murder following her first conviction.

Alvin Neelley died at the Bostick State Prison in November 2005.

Judith Neelley was on Alabama's Death Row at the Julia Tutwiler Prison for Women. She became the youngest woman sentenced to death in the United States.

Her appeal for a new trial was denied in 1987. The United States Supreme Court confirmed Neelley's death sentence in 1989. She was days from her execution date on January 15, 1999, when Alabama's then-governor Fob James gave her clemency. He commuted Neelley's death sentence to life in prison.

MEDIA

The Neelleys' case was described on the Investigation Discovery program "Most Evil" on February 28, 2008. Forensic psychiatrist Michael Stone developed a scale for serial torture murderers. According to it, Judith was ranked as a category 22 killer, the "most evil" level.

Judith and Alvin Neelley were featured on Wicked Attraction in the episode "Hearts of Darkness" on October 23, 2008.

In 2011, Judith was featured on "Deadly Women."

OUTCOME

Judith Neelley is currently imprisoned at Julia Tutwiler Prison for Women, Wetumpka, Alabama.

MARIE NOE

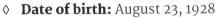

- ◊ **Date of birth:** August 23, 1928
- ◊ **Number of victims:** 8
- ◊ **Date of murders:** 1949 – 1968
- ◊ **Date of arrest:** August 1998
- ◊ **Murder method:** Suffocation with a pillow or other soft object
- ◊ **Known victims:** Eight of her children
- ◊ **Crime location:** Philadelphia, Pennsylvania, United States
- ◊ **Status:** Sentenced to 20 years of probation with the first five years under house arrest

BACKGROUND

Marie Noe's parents had a troubled marriage. Marie contracted scarlet fever at the age of five, which she later blamed as the cause of learning problems. When Noe was at her teens, she dropped out of school. She started work and helped to care for a niece, born to one of her older sisters when Marie was twelve.

Marie met her future husband, Arthur Noe, at a private club in the West Kensington neighborhood of Philadelphia. The couple eloped after a brief courtship. They proceeded to have ten children, all of whom died between the ages of five days and fourteen months: Richard Allan Noe (born March 7, 1949 – died April 7, 1949); Elizabeth Mary Noe (born September 8, 1950 – died February 17, 1951); Jacqueline Noe (born April 23, 1952 – died May 3, 1952); Arthur Joseph Jr. Noe (born April 23, 1955 – died April

28, 1955); Letitia Noe (stillborn, August 24, 1959; cause of death was umbilical cord knot); Constance Noe (born February 24, 1958 – died March 20, 1958); Mary Lee Noe (born June 19, 1962 – died January 4, 1963); Theresa Noe (died in hospital, June 1963; "congenital hemorrhagic diathesis" was the cause of her death); Catherine E. Noe (born December 3, 1964 – died February 24, 1966); Arthur Joseph Jr. Noe (born July 28, 1967 – died January 2, 1968).

During the Caesarean birth of the last child, Marie Noe suffered a uterine rupture and had a hysterectomy.

In 1997, interest in the case was resumed after the publication of the book The Death of Innocents, and an investigative article that appeared in the April 1998 issue of "Philadelphia" magazine.

MURDERS, ARREST, AND TRIAL

In March 1998, the author of the Philadelphia article turned over his investigation results to the Philadelphia Police Department. After receiving the material, the police questioned Mrs. Noe, who confessed to suffocating four of her children. She declared that she could not remember what happened to the other four children who died under similar circumstances.

In August 1998, the authorities charged her with first-degree murder. Mrs. Noe confessed to eight counts of second-degree murder. In June 1999, the judge sentenced her to twenty years of probation with the first five years under house arrest.

Noe also agreed to psychiatric study in hopes of clarifying what forced her to kill her children. A study was filed with the court in September 2001. It stated that Noe had a mixed personality disorder.

BOOKS

John Glatt wrote the book Cradle of Death, which is about Marie Noe and her children's murders. Many other books demonstrate Marie Noe alongside other criminals, such as Joseph W. Laythe's book Engendered Death: Pennsylvania Women Who Kill and Ron Franscell and Karen B. Valentine's book The Crime Buff's Guide to Outlaw Pennsylvania. Maribeth Fischer's fictional book The Life You Longed For: A Novel also mentions Noe's murders.

DIANE O'DELL

- ◊ **Date of birth:** 1953
- ◊ **Other names:** Infanticide
- ◊ **Number of victims:** 3 – 4
- ◊ **Date of murders:** 1982; 1983; 1985
- ◊ **Date of arrest:** May 17, 2003
- ◊ **Murder method:** Asphyxiation
- ◊ **Known victims:** Three of her newborn babies
- ◊ **Crime location:** Sullivan County, New York, United States
- ◊ **Status:** On January 28, 2004, sentenced to 25 years to life in state prison.

MURDERS, ARREST AND TRIAL

In May 2003, New York State Police charged that they had found the three dead infants in an abandoned storage unit in Arizona. They were born and killed in upstate Sullivan County.

They made the chilling claim on three counts of second-degree murder shortly after arresting Diane O'Dell, a former resident of Bethel.

According to police, forty-nine-year-old O'Dell moved from place to place across the country and carried the decaying corpses of the three infant babies with her.

In 1992, the bizarre odyssey ended when O'Dell settled in Arizona and stacked her infants' remains in a rental storage unit. The officials said that she then left town abruptly without picking them up.

According to Stephen Lungren, a Sullivan County District Attorney, her common-law husband, Robert Sauerstein, did not know about the grisly contents of the boxes that went with them during their frequent moves.

Lungren stated that the three infants were born between 1981 and 1984. During that time O'Dell was living in the hamlet of Kauneonga Lake, in Bethel Township, about 85 miles north of New York City.

O'Dell declared her three newborns died of natural causes shortly after their birth, but Lungen disputes this, "The babies were not stillborn. Our opinion is that the infants didn't die of accidental or natural causes."

Lungren said that O'Dell had kept the three pregnancies, and the births, a secret. She could hide her condition because she was very heavy. The police did not know who fathered the three infants, who were born between O'Dell's two long-term relationships. O'Dell had been married and had three children, but in 1981, she left them and her husband in Florida.

Lungren stated that in 1985, she hooked up with Sauerstein, with whom she had five children.

In 1989, Sullivan County authorities investigated O'Dell after the police discovered an infant's remains in a suitcase in a car. O'Dell gave birth to the baby in 1972.

The authorities did not file charges against her at the time; he said, "because it was unfounded as a criminal case. We believed the baby was stillborn, that it was born dead because O'Dell has been violently assaulted by her father and her father had since died."

In 1972, O'Dell was living at Kauneonga Lake in Sullivan County, N.Y. where she gave birth to a baby. She put it in a plastic bag and hid it in a suitcase.

In early 1981, she married and moved with her husband to Florida; then she left them and returned to Kauneonga. In 1981-1984 O'Dell, hiding her pregnancies, had three children in quick succession, each of them dying soon after birth. She packed their bodies in boxes and hid them too.

In 1985, O'Dell began living with Robert Sauerstein, who became her common-law husband and father of five of her children.

In 1989, Sullivan County authorities questioned O'Dell after they had found an infant's body in a suitcase in a car. She told them it was stillborn because of beatings from her father.

In 1991, O'Dell rented a storage unit to stow the boxes containing the remains of her three dead babies with other personal possessions in nearby Safford, Ariz.

In 1992, O'Dell and family suddenly picked up stakes after Sauerstein ran into trouble with local authorities. Their stored possessions were left behind.

In 1999, O'Dell stopped paying rent on the Arizona storage unit.

On May 12, 2003, the babies' remains were discovered after the contents of O'Dell's abandoned storage unit had been auctioned off for $75.

On May 20, 2003, O'Dell was questioned by New York state police and charged with three counts of second-degree murder.

Lungren said the police reopened that case. He said autopsies had been conducted on the remains of the three infants found in Arizona. State Police arrested O'Dell after interviewing her. O'Dell's court-appointed lawyer entered a plea of not guilty, but she was arraigned in Liberty Criminal Court and ordered held without bail.

State Police Major, Alan Martin, who announced the arrest said it was one of the most unusual cases in his law-enforcement career.

OUTCOME

In 2004, the officials sentenced O'Dell to life in prison. She will be eligible for parole in 2029.

LOUISE PEETE

- ◊ **Date of birth:** September 20, 1880
- ◊ **Other names:** Louise M. Gould, Anna Lee
- ◊ **Motive:** Financial gain
- ◊ **Number of victims:** 3+
- ◊ **Date of murders:** 1913, 1920, 1944
- ◊ **Date of arrest:** December 20, 1944
- ◊ **Murder method:** Shooting
- ◊ **Known victims:** Joe Appel, Jacob Charles Denton, Margaret Logan
- ◊ **Crime location:** Texas, California, United States
- ◊ **Status:** On April 11, 1947, executed in the California gas chamber.

BACKGROUND

Louise Peete was born Lofie Louise Preslar in Bienville, Louisiana. Her father was a wealthy newspaper publisher. Peete's family was quite wealthy, and she received an expensive education but was expelled from school for improper behavior. She married a traveling salesman Henry Bosley in 1903. Bosley committed suicide after discovering his wife with another man. She then worked as a high-class prostitute in Boston, stealing from her clients.

MURDERS

She moved to Waco, Texas, where she became involved with wealthy oil baron Joe Appel who was found murdered. His jewelry was missing. A grand jury accused her of his murder, but she convinced them that she had defended herself from violence.

In 1913, she married Harry Faurote, a hotel clerk. After finding her with another man, he committed suicide.

She married a salesman, Richard Peete, in 1915, in Denver. The couple had a daughter, but Peete left them and moved to Los Angeles. She began living with Jacob C. Denton, an oil magnate. In 1920, Denton disappeared. By the time the police searched Denton's house, Peete had escaped to her husband in Denver. The police officers found Denton's body, and the authorities charged Peete with his murder. On February 17, 1921, the judge sentenced her to life imprisonment. During the first two years of Peete's sentence, her husband Richard still believed she was innocent. She told Richard to divorce her, so he would be free to marry again. Soon after the divorce, Peete stopped answering his letters and refused to see him. Despondent over her rejection, her husband shot himself.

Peete was released after serving 18 years. She worked as a housekeeper for a woman named Jessie Marcy, who died not long afterward. Peete's elderly co-worker also died under suspicious circumstances.

Emily Dwight Latham had helped to secure Peete's parole. Peete then worked for her. Latham also died. The authorities assigned the deaths of Marcy and Latham to natural causes.

Peete then became a housekeeper for Arthur C. Logan and his wife Margaret in Pacific Palisades, California. She married a man named Lee Borden Judson. Soon Margaret Logan disappeared. Three days later, Arthur was brought to Patton State Hospital by Peete. When neighbors asked about Margaret's whereabouts, Peete stated that Arthur had attacked his wife and bitten her nose severely. Peete added that Margaret had gone to undergo plastic surgery. Peete and her husband lived in the Logans' home. On December 6, 1944, Arthur died in Patton State Hospital. Peete donated his body to science. She presented poor forgeries of her signature on checks and letters to her parole officer. It aroused suspicion and employees at the Logans' bank called the police.

ARREST AND TRIAL

The police officers searched the Logan home. Six months after Margaret disappeared, on December 20, 1944, police discovered her decomposing body buried in the backyard. Peete was arrested and charged with the murder. During questioning, Peete claimed that Margaret was beaten and shot by her husband during a "homicidal frenzy." Peete denied killing her but admitted that she buried Margaret. She explained she did not report the murder because of fear she would be blamed due to her previous conviction. An autopsy showed that Margaret had been shot in the back of the neck and had gotten a skull fracture.

The police also arrested Judson and charged him with murder. On January 11, 1945, the authorities acquitted Judson of involvement, but he committed suicide the day after he spoke to police. He jumped from the ninth floor of the Spring Arcade, an office building in Los Angeles.

On April 23, 1945, Peete's third murder trial began in Los Angeles. Prosecutors assumed that Peete murdered Margaret Logan to gain control of her money. A jury announced Louise Peete guilty of first-degree murder and sentenced her to death on May 31. While the prosecutor was reading her sentence, Peete sat in the courtroom reading a Chinese philosophy book The Importance of Living by Lin Yutang.

OUTCOME

Peete continued to insist on her innocence. She filed several appeals, but they failed. On April 11, 1947, Peete was executed in the gas chamber at San Quentin State Prison at age 66. Louise Peete is buried at Angelus-Rosedale Cemetery in Los Angeles.

DOROTHEA PUENTE

- ◊ **Date of birth:** January 9, 1929
- ◊ **Nicknames:** Death House Landlady
- ◊ **Motive:** She cashed the Social Security checks
- ◊ **Number of victims:** 9 – 15
- ◊ **Date of murders:** 1982 – 1988
- ◊ **Date of arrest:** November 17, 1988
- ◊ **Murder method:** Poisoning (drug overdose)
- ◊ **Known victims:** Ruth Munroe, 61; Everson Gillmouth, 77; Alvaro "Bert" Montoya, 51; Dorothy Miller, 64; Benjamin Fink, 55; Betty Palmer, 78; Leona Carpenter, 78; James Gallop, 62; Vera Faye Martin, 64.
- ◊ **Crime location:** Sacramento, California, United States
- ◊ **Status:** On March 27, 2011, she died in prison.

BACKGROUND

Dorothea Helen Puente was born Dorothea Helen Gray in Redlands, California on January 9, 1929. Her parents were Trudy Mae Yates and Jesse James Gray. They worked as cotton pickers. In 1937, when she was eight, her father died of tuberculosis. A year later her mother died in a motorcycle accident. The authorities sent her to an orphanage until relatives from Fresno, California, took her in.

In 1945, at the age of 16, she married a soldier named Fred McFaul. He had just returned from the Pacific Theater. They had two daughters between 1946 and 1948, but she decided to send one to her relatives in Sacramento. The other was given up for adoption.

In 1948, Dorothea became pregnant again but suffered a miscarriage. McFaul left her in late 1948. She tried to forge checks, but the police caught her, and she was sentenced to a year in jail. After six months, she was paroled. Soon after her release, Dorothea gave birth to a daughter, whom she gave up for adoption. She married a Swede named Axel Johanson in 1952, and the couple had a turbulent fourteen-year union.

In 1960, the authorities arrested her for owning and managing a brothel. They sentenced her to ninety days in the County Jail. Soon after the release, she was arrested for vagrancy and sentenced to another ninety days in jail. Dorothea began a career of a criminal, and over time the crimes became more serious. She began to work as a nurse, caring for disabled and older adults in private homes. She soon started managing boarding houses.

In 1966, she divorced Johansen and married Roberto Puente, a man nineteen years her junior. Their marriage lasted only two years. After divorce, Dorothea Puente took over a three-story, sixteen-bedroom care home in Sacramento, California.

In 1976, Puente married for the fourth time to a violent alcoholic, Pedro Montalvo. After a few months, they divorced. Puente spent time in local bars. She was looking for older men who were receiving benefits. Puente forged their signatures to use their money, but police officers caught her again, and she was charged with thirty-four counts of treasury falsification. According to records from California Court of Appeal, in 1981 Puente rented an upstairs apartment in downtown Sacramento. In 1988, she was charged with nine murders which were associated with this upstairs apartment and not her previous sixteen-room boarding house.

MURDERS

Puente had a mixed reputation in the boarding house. Some residents rebelled against her avarice and blamed her for stealing their mail or money. Other tenants praised her for small acts of kindness or her sumptuous home-made food. Puente killed tenants for money. Police estimated her ill-gotten income was more than $5,000 per month.

In April 1982, Ruth Monroe, a sixty-one-year-old friend, and a business partner began living with Puente in her upstairs apartment. She soon died from an overdose of Tylenol and codeine. Puente told the police officers that the woman was deeply depressed because her husband was seriously ill. They believed her and judged the incident suicide.

A few weeks later, the police returned after a seventy-four-year-old pensioner named Malcolm McKenzie blamed Puente for drugging and stealing from him.

On August 18, 1982, she was convicted of three charges of theft, and sentenced to five years in jail. Being in prison, she began corresponding with a seventy-seven-year-old retiree named Everson Gillmouth. He was living in Oregon. In 1985, Puente was released. She served just three years of her sentence. Gillmouth was waiting for her in a red Ford pickup. They opened a joint bank account and paid monthly rent for the upstairs apartment in Sacramento. The couple was making wedding plans.

Puente hired handyman Ismael Florez in November 1985. She asked him to build a box in her apartment to store "books and other items." For his labor, Puente gave him a red Ford pickup in good condition. With Florez Puente, she transported the box--which was filled and nailed-shut--to a warehouse. On the way, however, she asked him to stop and dump the box on the river bank, explaining that the contents of the box were rubbish.

On January 1, 1986, a fisherman saw the box on the bank of the river and called the police. The police officers found a badly decomposed and unidentifiable body of an elderly man inside. Puente collected Gillmouth's pension and sent letters to his family, writing that the reason he had not contacted them was his illness. For three years, Gillmouth's body remained unidentified.

Puente continued to accept elderly tenants. She was popular with local social workers because she took "tough cases," including abusive tenants and drug addicts. During this period, parole agents visited Puente, and they did not note any violations.

Neighbors noticed strange activities of a homeless alcoholic woman known as Chief, and the first suspicion was aroused. The "Chief" dug in the basement, carted soil and rubbish away in a wheelbarrow. Soon afterward, Chief disappeared.

ARREST AND TRIAL

On November 11, 1988, a social worker told the police about the disappearance of tenant Alvaro Montoya, a developmentally disabled schizophrenic. The investigators uncovered the body of seventy-eight-years-old tenant Leona Carpenter after

noticing disturbed soil on Puente's property. They also found seven other bodies. The authorities charged Puente with a total of nine murders. She was convicted of three of them and sentenced to two life sentences.

Her trial began in October 1992 and ended in 1993. The prosecutor, John O'Mara, called over 130 witnesses. The jury discussed the case for over a month and found Puente guilty of three murders. They could not agree on the others.

Dorothea Puente received life without the possibility of parole under the law. She was imprisoned at Central California Women's Facility in Chowchilla, Madera County, California. She maintained her innocence for the rest of her life and insisted all her tenants had died of "natural causes."

OUTCOME

On March 27, 2011, she died from natural causes in prison at the age of eighty-two.

TERRI RACHALS

- ◊ **Date of birth:** 1961
- ◊ **Nicknames:** Angel of Death
- ◊ **Number of victims:** 6 – 9
- ◊ **Date of murders:** August – December 1985
- ◊ **Date of arrest:** March 13, 1986
- ◊ **Murder method:** Poisoning (by injecting lethal doses of potassium chloride)
- ◊ **Victims:** Seriously ill patients
- ◊ **Crime location:** Albany, Georgia, United States
- ◊ **Status:** Released on April 1, 2003.

MURDERS

In November 1985, administrators at Phoebe Putney Hospital, in Albany, Georgia, were alarmed by a sudden rash of cardiac arrests in the intensive care unit. A review of hospital records showed six suspicious deaths, with an equal number of near-misses, since late October. The administrators notified the police. Post-mortem examinations blamed the six deaths on injections of potassium chloride, and homicide investigators went to work on the case full-time.

Sixty-eight-year-old Milton Lucas had been the first apparent victim, declared dead on October 19, 1985. Lost on November 7, Minnie Houck, age 58, was next; 36-year-old Joe Irwin joined the list three days later. On November 15, Roger Parker, also 36, died; 73-year-old Andrew Daniels lost his struggle for life on November 24. Two days later three-year-old Norris Morgan followed him. Some patients survived. They included Frances Freeman, George Whiting, Jack Stephens, and Sam Bentley. They all had suffered one or more inexplicable cardiac arrests.

The authorities were confident of six victims by New Years. There may have been more. A 26-year-old jail inmate Lee Creech had died on December 21. Detectives became suspicious of four other deaths, dating back to mid-August.

ARREST AND TRIAL

By March, the investigation had concentrated on a nurse, Terri Eden Maples Rachals, age 24, who confessed on March 13 to injecting lethal doses of potassium chloride to her patients.

On March 25, 1986, the authorities indicted Rachals on six counts of murder and twenty counts of aggravated assault against nine patients. Some of her patients had received multiple injections. Creech and Parker held the record at six and four jolts.

At September trial, the prosecution declared that Rachals felt like a second-class citizen all her life. She craved power and control that she ultimately gained by murdering patients.

On September 23, Terri recanted her statements of confessions, denying her attacks.

The jury reached a verdict of guilty but mentally ill on one count of aggravated assault on September 26. They acquitted Rachals on all other charges. Jurors stated that, while she may have been responsible for several deaths, the prosecution had not proved the case.

On October 1, the authorities sentenced Rachals to a 17-year prison term, with three years of probation on release.

OUTCOME

After serving seventeen years in prison, Rachals was released in 2003.

KIMBERLY CLARK SAENZ

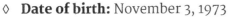

- ◊ **Date of birth:** November 3, 1973
- ◊ **Other names:** Kimberly Clark Fowler
- ◊ **Number of victims:** 5
- ◊ **Date of murders:** January–April 2008
- ◊ **Date of arrest:** 2008
- ◊ **Murder method:** Poisoning by injecting their bloodstreams with bleach
- ◊ **Known victims:** Kidney dialysis patients: Clara Strange, Thelma Metcalf, Garlin Kelley, Cora Bryant, Opal Few
- ◊ **Crime location:** Texas, United States
- ◊ **Status:** On April 2, 2012, sentenced to life imprisonment with no eligibility for parole.

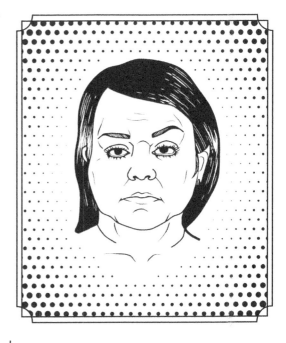

BACKGROUND

In 2008, 34-year-old Kimberly Clark Saenz was a licensed practical nurse. At the time of the murders, she was married and had two young children. She suffered from substance dependence and used stolen prescription medication. Saenz had been fired four times from health care jobs. She placed disinformation on an application for employment and looked for a health care job in breach of the terms of her bail.

ARREST AND TRIAL

On March 31, 2012, the Texas District Court found a nurse, Kimberly Clark Saenz, guilty of murders of five kidney dialysis patients and injuring five other patients. The Angelina County jury sentenced her to life imprisonment on April 2, 2012, with no eligibility for parole and three twenty-year sentences for aggravated assault.

Clara Strange, Thelma Metcalf, Cora Bryant, Garlin Kelley and Opal Few were the five murder victims.

The two eyewitnesses Leraline Hamilton and Linda Hall confirmed that on April 28, 2008, Saenz drew sodium hypochlorite, known as bleach, into syringes and injected the substance into two patient's dialysis lines.

The Drug Administration prepared a document proving that samples of some victims of violence tested positive for bleach when others indicated bleach present at one time.

Law enforcement officers at Lufkin dialysis clinic testified at the trial that they arrested Saenz for public intoxication and criminal trespass. She also had domestic disturbances with her husband, Mark Kevin Saenz. He had filed for divorce and had obtained a restraining order against his former wife in June 2007, one year before the clinic illnesses and deaths.

The trial records reflected that before working at DaVita clinic, the head Woodland Heights hospital had fired Saenz for stealing Demerol. In April 2008, Saenz was fired from DaVita following numerous deaths at the clinic. Her nursing license was suspended. She then applied to work as a receptionist in a Lufkin medical office and lied on her job application about previous employment.

At the trial the daughter of the victim, Thelma Metcalf told Saenz that she was nothing more than a psychopathic serial killer and Thelma hoped Saenz would burn in hell.

The prosecutor, Clyde Herrington, based on the research of the epidemiologist from the Centers for Disease Control and Prevention, believed there were more victims than just the ten indicted cases. The epidemiologist connected Saenz to other adverse health events to patients. Before April 28, 2008, Lufkin Police detectives could only obtain the medical waste from two weeks, so there was not enough evidence to raise further bills of indictment against Saenz in the other incidents.

OUTCOME

Saenz's defense team is planning to appeal to the Twelfth Court of Appeal of Texas. Saenz is currently serving her sentence at Mountain View Unit.

LYDIA SHERMAN

- ◊ **Date of birth:** December 24, 1824
- ◊ **Nicknames:** The Derby Poisoner
- ◊ **Motive:** Life insurance
- ◊ **Number of victims:** 12
- ◊ **Date of murders:** 1863 – 1877
- ◊ **Date of arrest:** June 7, 1872
- ◊ **Murder method:**
  Poisoning (arsenic)
- ◊ **Known victims:** Her first husband
  Edward Struck; her daughter
  Martha Struck, 6; her son William
  Struck, 9 months; her son Edward
  Struck Jr., almost 4; her second
  husband, Dennis Hurlburt; third
  husband Horatio N. Sherman;
  her stepdaughter Ada Sherman;
  her stepson Frankie Sherman.
- ◊ **Crime location:** New York, New
  Jersey, Connecticut, United States
- ◊ **Status:** In 1872, sentenced
  to life in prison. Died in
  prison on May 16, 1878.

BACKGROUND, MURDERS

In the 1870s Lydia Sherman was found to be one of the most cold-hearted and successful poisoners to come out of nineteenth-century America.

The story begins in the early 1860s. Lydia was married to, paradoxically enough, a policeman named Edward Struck. Edward and Lydia had six children. One day, according to Lydia, it had all become too much.

She decided to put an end to any more pregnancies. Lydia purchased some Rat Poison at the chemist. Then, feeling she could make some money out of her plan, insured her husband's life for a small sum.

Lydia's husband died quickly, and nobody had any suspicions. So, she insured and murdered all six of her children, leaving her wealthy and free. Sherman was a skilled actress, for no one ever thought of her as being anything but a poor widow.

In 1868, Lydia married Dennis Hurlburt, a prosperous farmer from New Haven, Connecticut. Some said that he was senile. By 1870, Lydia was not only a widow again, but had wasted most of Dennis's estate.

In April 1870, she took a job as housekeeper to Nelson Sherman, who had lost his wife and needed someone to look after his baby son and fourteen-year-old daughter.

Nelson and Lydia grew close, and soon, he agreed to marry her. In gratitude, Lydia poisoned, with arsenic, his son and daughter. Nelson Sherman was grief-stricken at the loss of his children. In May 1871, he succumbed to a poisoned hot chocolate drink.

This time Lydia's luck ran out. Dr. Beardsly smelled a rat and ordered a second opinion, and then a third. The bodies of the children were exhumed, and Dr. Beardsly's suspicions of poisoning by arsenic were proved.

ARREST AND TRIAL

Dr. Beardsley notified the police, but Lydia had fled to New York. The authorities ordered Mrs. Sherman's extradition back to Connecticut to face trial.

Lydia Sherman was convicted of second-degree murder and sentenced to life imprisonment.

OUTCOME

On May 16, 1878, Lydia Sherman died of cancer in prison.

LYDA SOUTHARD

◊ **Date of birth:** October 16, 1892
◊ **Nicknames:** Flypaper Lyda, The Black Widow
◊ **Motive:** Life insurance
◊ **Number of victims:** 6
◊ **Date of murders:** 1915 – 1920
◊ **Date of arrest:** May 1921
◊ **Murder method:** Arsenic poisoning
◊ **Known victims:** Her brother-in-law, four husbands, and a daughter
◊ **Crime location:** Idaho, Montana, United States
◊ **Status:** Paroled on October 3, 1941. Died on February 5, 1958.

BACKGROUND

On October 16, 1892, Lydia Keller was born in Keytesville, Missouri. In 1906, The Trueblood family moved to Twin Falls, Idaho.

MARRIAGES

On March 17, 1912, Lyda Anna Mae Trueblood married Robert Dooley. They settled with his brother Ed Dooley on a ranch in Twin Falls, Idaho. In 1914, the couple had a daughter, Lorraine who died unexpectedly in 1915. Lyda claimed that it was a result of drinking water from a dirty well. Soon afterward, in August 1915, Edward Dooley died. The cause of death was ptomaine poisoning. On October 12, 1915, Robert Dooley fell ill and died of typhoid fever. Shortly after their death, Lyda collected on the life insurance policies of each person.

Within two years of Robert's death, Lyda met and married William G. McHaffle. In a little while, Lyda's three-year-old daughter fell ill and died, and the McHaffles moved to Montana. A year later, McHaffle suddenly fell ill. Doctors thought it was influenza and diphtheria. On October 1, 1918, McHaffle died in Montana.

She married an automobile salesman from Billings, Montana, Harlen C. Lewis, in March 1919. Within four months of the marriage, Lewis began to feel sick and soon died from complications of gastroenteritis.

In August 1920, Lyda married for a fourth time in Pocatello, Idaho, to Edward F. Meyer, a ranch foreman. He soon fell ill of typhoid and died on September 7, 1920.

MURDERS

A relative of Lyda's first husband, Twin Falls chemist Earl Dooley, began to study the deaths surrounding her. His helpers were a physician and another chemist, and they soon found out that Ed and Bob Dooley had been murdered by poisoning with arsenic. Frank Stephan, Twin Falls County Prosecutor, began an investigation and started exhuming the bodies of three of Lyda's husbands, her brother-in-law, and a 4-year-old daughter. Stephan discovered that some of the bodies had traces of arsenic. He also found Lyda's motive in the records of the Idaho State Life Insurance company of Boise. All four of her husbands had held a life insurance policy where they listed her as the beneficiary.

This time Lyda was found by law enforcement in Honolulu, married for the fifth time to Navy officer Paul Southard. The authorities deported her to Idaho where she was arraigned on June 11, 1921.

ARREST AND TRIAL

After a six-week trial, she was convicted of second-degree murder and sentenced to ten years to life imprisonment in the Old Idaho State Prison. On May 4, 1931, she escaped from prison. Lyda took up residence in Denver, Colorado where she worked as a housekeeper for Harry Whitlock. They married in March 1932. On July 31, 1932, Whitlock ultimately assisted in her arrest in Topeka, Kansas. In August 1932, she returned to jail. In October 1941, Lyda was released on probation, and in 1942 received a final pardon. Following the return to Idaho, Lyda faced murder charges on Meyer. In court, she pled not guilty but was convicted of arsenic murders of her husbands. The judge sentenced her to ten years to life in an Idaho prison. It was determined that her motive for the murders was money since she collected on her dead husbands' life insurance policies.

OUTCOME

On February 5, 1958, Lyda died of a heart attack in Salt Lake City, Utah. Her body was buried at Sunset Memorial Park in Twin Falls, Idaho.

GEORGIA TANN

- ◊ **Date of birth:** July 18, 1891
- ◊ **Other names:** Beulah George Tann
- ◊ **Motive:** Profit
- ◊ **Number of victims:** 19+
- ◊ **Date of murders:** 1924 – 1950
- ◊ **Date of arrest:** Died before arrest
- ◊ **Murder method:** Starvation
- ◊ **Crime location:** Tennessee, United States
- ◊ **Status:** Died of cancer before arrest.

BACKGROUND

Georgia Tann was born in Philadelphia, Mississippi on July 18, 1891. Her father was George Clark Tann, who was a district court judge. Her mother was Beulah Isabella Yates. She had a younger brother, Rob Roy Tann. Judge Tann reportedly had a domineering personality. He dreamed of his daughter becoming a concert pianist and started her piano lessons when she was five. Georgia attended Martha Washington College in Abingdon, Virginia, graduating with a degree in music in 1913. She also took social courses for two summers at Columbia University in New York. She, however, despised playing piano and, instead, desired to become a lawyer as her father had been. Under her father's tutelage, Georgia read the law and passed the state bar exam in Mississippi. Her father, however, did not want her to practice law because it was unusual for women. Georgia did not want to get married or have children. She got one of the careers available to unmarried women of her time, social work.

ILLEGAL LIFE

In 1924, Tann moved to Memphis, Tennessee with her adopted daughter, June, and her girlfriend, Ann Atwood. Atwood had given birth to an illegitimate son, and around this time appended Hollinsworth to her name to give the impression that she had been widowed. While "Boston marriages," or cohabitation of two financially independent women, had been socially acceptable, such arrangements had been viewed as homosexual. Tann and Atwood tried not to show the true nature of their relationship.

In Memphis, Tann began trafficking children. This time adoption was a rare practice in the United States, with the

Boston Children's Aid Society placing five children per year. For comparison, Tann placed 206 children with adoptive families in 1928.

Tann used various methods to get children. She would coerce or dupe birth parents, mostly poor single mothers, to turn the children over to her custody through pressure tactics, threats of legal action, and many other ways. In turn, Tann might sell the children to her rich patrons.

Tann also organized, through her connections, the taking of children born to inmates at Tennessee mental institutions. She soon resorted to kidnappings to meet demand.

In some cases, single parents dropped their children off at nursery schools and were later told that social agents had taken their children. In others, children were placed in an orphan home because a family was experiencing illness or unemployment, but later, the family would find out that the orphanage had adopted their children out.

Tann took children born to unwed mothers at birth, stating that newborns needed medical care. When the mothers asked about their children, Tann or her accomplices would explain that the babies had died.

Tann did not care about the children, and she mistreated them with reports of neglect, physical abuse, sexual abuse, and murder. In the nation, Memphis had the highest infant mortality rate in the 1930s. Some children were never buried or accounted for, and the exact numbers of deceased children remain unknown.

Memphis Family Court Judge Camille Kelley accomplished Tann's crimes. The Judge used her position to sanction Tann's activities and tactics. Kelley severed custody of divorced mothers, placing the children with Tann, who then arranged for the adoption of the children into "better homes." However, she placed many of the children into homes with abusive families or where they were used as child labor on farms.

Tann falsified medical histories of the children and conducted minimal background checks on the adoptive parents. She also fictionalized many of the files of the children before presenting to the adoptive parents. As a result, in 1941, the Child Welfare League of America dropped the Society from its list of qualifying institutions.

On August 2, 1943, Tann adopted Hollinsworth, in Dyer County, Tennessee.

The Georgia Tann/Tennessee Children's Home scandal resulted in adoption reform laws in Tennessee in 1951.

Tennessee law permitted agencies to charge the appropriate applicants for the services to ban the selling of children. According to the law, the Home charged about $7 per adoption. Tann, however, also had arranged for out-of-state private adoptions where she charged a premium, upwards of $5,000 per child. Additionally, Tann charged prospective parents for background checks she never fulfilled, air travel costs at excessive rates, and adoption paperwork more expensive than the real price. Tann kept her profits in a secret bank account under a false name at the time.

In 1950, the authorities closed The Tennessee Children's Home Society.

Tann made millions selling children,

ninety percent of them to people in New York and California.

Actress Joan Crawford used Tann's services. Her twin daughters, Cathy and Cynthia, were adopted through the agency. Notable personalities who also used the services of the Memphis-based home for adopting a child included June Allyson and husband, Dick Powell. In 1935, New York Governor Herbert Lehman signed a law sealing birth certificates from New York adoptees. He also adopted a child through the agency.

Tann is alleged to have stolen over 5,000 children. Over several decades, Tann buried nineteen of the children who died at the Tennessee Children's Home Society in a 14 ft × 13 ft lot at the historic Elmwood Cemetery with no headstones. Sometime before 1923, Tann bought the lot and recorded the children there by their first names. The cemetery erected a monument to their memory in 2015. It reads, "In memory of the 19 children who finally rest here unmarked if not unknown, and of all the hundreds who died under the cold, hard hand of the Tennessee Children's Home Society."

MEDIA

The scandal was the subject of two films: Missing Children: A Mother's Story (1982), and Stolen Babies (1993). On September 13, 2013, the subject of Georgia Tann aired in an episode of Investigation Discovery's series Deadly Women titled "Above the Law" and appeared on an episode of Unsolved Mysteries. She appears in several episodes: the April 25, 2017, the podcast Southern Hollows; the August 29, 2017, the True Crime Brewery podcast titled "The Baby Thief: The Crimes of Georgia Tann"; the March 15, 2019, the Criminal podcast titled "Baby Snatcher," and the April 30, 2019 two-part episode of the Behind The Bastards podcast titled "The Woman Who Invented Adoption By Stealing Thousands of Babies."

OUTCOME

In 1950, Tann died. She was buried in Hickory Cemetery.

MARYBETH TINNING

- ◊ **Date of birth:** September 11, 1942
- ◊ **Other names:** Murderous Mom, Notorious Child Killer, Schenectady Child Killer
- ◊ **Motive:** She would murder her kids so that she could get sympathy from others.
- ◊ **Number of victims:** 8
- ◊ **Date of murders:** 1972 – 1985
- ◊ **Date of arrest:** December 20, 1985
- ◊ **Murder method:** Pillow (smothering)
- ◊ **Known victims:** Her children
- ◊ **Crime location:** Schenectady County, New York, United States
- ◊ **Status:** On October 1, 1987, sentenced to 20 years to life in prison. On August 21, 2018, Tinning was released on parole.

BACKGROUND

Marybeth Roe was born in Duanesburg, New York on September 11, 1942 to Ruth and Alton Lewis Roe. During a portion of her formative years, her father was fighting in World War II while her mother was working. Marybeth was shuffled between nearby relatives for care due to both of her parents being away at times. Once one of her elderly relatives told her she was an accidental child and her birth was unwanted. When her little brother reached adolescence, Marybeth said to him that he was the one their parents wanted, not her.

Her father on completion of his active duty worked as a press operator in a nearby General Electric facility. Marybeth later claimed that when she was a child, her father abused her. In 1986, during a police interview, she told an investigator that her father had beaten her and locked in a closet.

Marybeth studied at Duanesburg High School. She was an average student and graduated from the high school in 1961. After school, Marybeth worked at various low-paying and unskilled jobs. One day, she settled on a job as a nursing assistant at Ellis Hospital in Schenectady, New York.

In 1963, she met Joseph Tinning who was very quiet and lighthearted. In 1965, the pair married. In May 1967, Marybeth gave birth to their first child, Barbara. The Tinnings' second child, Joseph, was born in January 1970.

Joseph Tinning Sr. was admitted to the hospital in 1974. The doctors examined him and found he had a near-fatal dosage of barbiturate poisoning. Later Marybeth acknowledged that when this incident occurred, they had difficult times and were on the verge of divorce. This led to her placing pills into Joseph's juice. Joseph did not press charges against his wife.

MURDERS

In December 1971, Marybeth gave birth to their third child Jennifer. Eight-days-old Jennifer died from multiple brain abscesses and hemorrhagic meningitis. On January 20, 1972, Marybeth took her two-year-old son, Joseph Jr., to the Ellis Hospital emergency room. Doctors attributed his death to cardiopulmonary arrest. In two weeks, Marybeth took Barbara to the hospital because she was suffering from convulsions. The next day Barbara died. Doctors identified her death as Reye syndrome. Marybeth Tinning was 29. On Thanksgiving Day 1973, Tinnings' fourth baby, Timothy, was born. On December 10, Timothy was dead. Doctors defined his death as sudden infant death syndrome. In March 1975, Tinning gave birth to their fifth child, Nathan. He died in the Tinning's car while out with his mother that autumn.

Surprisingly, the Tinnings adopted Michael shortly after he was born in August 1978. On October 29, Marybeth gave birth to their sixth child, Mary Frances. Tinning rushed Mary Frances directly across the street from her apartment to the emergency room in January 1979. The staff revived her, reporting "aborted SIDS." Only one

month later, Marybeth returned to the hospital with her daughter in full cardiac arrest. The staff was again able to revive her, but the baby had severe brain damage. Two days later, Mary Frances died. In the fall, Tinning gave birth to their eighth child, Jonathan who died in a hospital in Albany, New York in March 1980.

In February, adopted Michael had been taken to the hospital because of a fall down the stairs. In March 1981, Tinning took him to the doctor's office because he would not wake up. Michael died. Since he was adopted, the long-suspected theory that the deaths in the Tinning family had a genetic origin was rejected.

In August 1985, Tinning gave birth to Tami Lynne. On December 20, the baby died from being smothered. That day, Betsy Mannix of Schenectady County's Department of Social Services together with Bob Imfeld of the Schenectady Police Department visited the Tinning family on the death of Tami Lynne.

The doctors listed the causes of the children's deaths as sudden infant death syndrome, natural or undetermined. Six autopsies were performed after Tami Lynne's death. Although no signs of abuse were found, there were suspicions of foul play.

ARREST AND TRIAL

Regarding the death of Tami Lynne, both parents, Marybeth and Joe Tinning, were separately taken to the Schenectady Police Department for interrogation. During the police questioning, Marybeth signed a confession to the murders of Timothy, Nathan, and Tami Lynne. The authorities arrested Marybeth and charged her with the murder of Tami Lynne.

In the beginning, police officials suspected that Tami Lynne died of SIDS but the lead forensic pathologist, Dr. Michael M. Baden, determined the cause of Tami Lynne's death was smothering. After charging Marybeth with Tami Lynne's death, authorities said that they considered the deaths of the eight other Tinning children to be suspicious. Investigators said that Jennifer's death was not suspect because it happened before the baby left the hospital.

Marybeth Tinning paid her $100,000 bail and was released until her trial date.

On June 22, 1987, Schenectady County Court began the murder trial of Tinning. Tami Lynne's pediatrician, Dr. Bradley Ford, witnessed on behalf of the prosecution, saying Tinning had discarded his suggestion to install an alarm device enabling the monitoring of the baby's breathing and heart rate due to her sibling's deaths. Two more prosecution witnesses, Dr. Marie Valdes-Dapena of Miami, president of the SIDS Foundation, and Dr. Thomas Oram, who performed the baby's autopsy, said they detected that Tami Lynne was smothered with a soft object.

After the six-week trial, the jury's deliberation led to the conviction of 44-year-old Tinning to one count of second-degree murder. As the judge Clifford Harrigan announced the verdict, Tinning placed her hands over her eyes and sobbed quietly.

After the trial, Tinning received a sentence of twenty years to life and was imprisoned at the Bedford Hills Correctional Facility for Women.

After her conviction, she appealed because she did not give her confession voluntarily and the officials did not have enough evidence for her conviction. In 1988, the New York State Supreme Court's Appellate Division denied her appeal.

In March 2007, Tinning's made her first attempt for parole. At the parole board hearing, Tinning stated, "I must be honest, and the only thing that I can tell you is that I know that my daughter is dead. I live with it every day. I have no recollection, and I can't believe that I harmed her. I can't say any more than that." The board denied her parole.

Tinning's second attempt for parole was in January 2009. The board again denied her parole.

At the 2011 parole board meeting, Tinning said: "After the deaths of my other children, I just lost it. I became a damaged worthless piece of a person, and when my daughter was young, in my state of mind at that time, I just believed that she was going to die also. So, I just did it."

Due to her lack of remorse, she was denied parole again.

In February 2015, Tinning went before the parole board again.

The parole board denied Tinning's release, explaining that she demonstrated no remorse nor any understanding for taking her baby's life. In January 2017, Tinning was denied parole for the sixth time.

On August 21, 2018, 76-year-old Tinning was released on parole. Before being granted parole, she served more than 31 years of her 20-years-to-life sentence. Tinning will stay under parole supervision for the rest of her life as part of the release. She must attend domestic violence counseling and has a curfew.

BOOKS

On July 19, 2011, the book The Killer, written by detective Mark Gado, was released.

In 1990, the book From Cradle to Grave: The Short Lives and Strange Deaths of Marybeth Tinning's Nine Children, written by an investigative author Joyce Egginton, detailed the case.

The book Unnatural Death, Confessions of a Forensic Pathologist, authored by Michael M. Baden with Judith Adler Hennessee was released in 1989.

MEDIA

In 1994, the Home Box Office network reported the Tinning case on the first episode of the crime documentary series Autopsy – Confessions of a Medical Examiner.

On March 7, 2007, the Investigation Discovery network covered Tinning's case in the forensic series Most Evil sub-titled "Most Evil – Murderous Women."

On November 4, 2011, the Investigation Discovery network released one more episode, via the documentary drama series Deadly Women, showing the tragedies that each of her children experienced. It is sub-titled "Deadly Women – Sacrifice Their Blood."

JANE TOPPAN

- ◊ **Date of birth:** August 17, 1854
- ◊ **Nicknames:** Jolly Jane, Angel of Death
- ◊ **Motive:** Derived a sexual thrill from patients being near death, coming back to life and then dying again
- ◊ **Number of victims:** 31+
- ◊ **Date of murders:** 1895 – 1901
- ◊ **Date of arrest:** October 29, 1901
- ◊ **Murder method:** Administered a drug mixture (morphine, atropine, and strychnine) to her patients
- ◊ **Known victims:** Her landlord, Israel Dunham, and his wife; her foster sister Elizabeth Brigham; the elderly Alden Davis and his wife, Mattie
- ◊ **Crime location:** Massachusetts, United States
- ◊ **Status:** She was found not guilty because of insanity and committed for life in the Taunton Insane Hospital where she died on October 29, 1938.

BACKGROUND

Jane Toppan was born Honora Kelly on August 17, 1854. Her parents were Irish immigrants. Her mother's name was Bridget Kelley. She died of tuberculosis when she was very young. Her father, Peter Kelley, was an alcoholic and known to be very abusive, and eccentric, nicknamed by those who knew him "Kelley, the Crack."

In 1863, Kelley took his two youngest children, eight-year-old Delia Josephine, and six-year-old Honora, to the Boston Female Asylum, an orphanage for indigent female children. Kelley gave the two girls away, never to see them again. Documents from the asylum note that the girls were saved from a very miserable home.

Mrs. Ann C. Toppan of Lowell, Massachusetts took Honora Kelley as an indentured servant in her home in November 1864. The Toppans never formally adopted Honora, but she took on the surname of her patrons and became known as Toppan. The Toppan family already had a daughter, Elizabeth; she and Toppan got along.

MURDERS

Toppan worked at Cambridge Hospital in 1885. She trained to be a nurse there.

Kelley had a lot of friends there and was well-liked. In her early years, she was described as brilliant and terrible, but at the hospital, she was well-liked, bright, friendly and nicknamed "Jolly Jane." Once Toppan became close with the elderly, and very sick patients, she picked her favorite ones. During her residency, she performed experiments with morphine and atropine using her patients as guinea pigs. Toppan changed their prescribed dosages to observe what could happen to their nervous systems; however, she spent a lot of time alone with patients, making up false charts and treating them to come to consciousness and lose it again. She even got into bed with her patients.

In 1889, the Cambridge Hospital officials recommended her for the prestigious Massachusetts General Hospital. There, she medicated several more victims before being dismissed the following year. She returned to Cambridge, but the officials soon fired her for administering opiates imprudently. She then began her work as a private nurse. Toppan flourished despite complaints of minor theft.

In 1895, she began her poisoning spree in earnest by killing her landlord, Israel Dunham, and his wife, Lovely Dunham. Toppan also killed her foster sister Elizabeth with a dose of strychnine in 1899. Jane moved in with an older man, Alden Davis, and his family in 1901. She took care of him after the death of his wife, Mattie, whom Toppan had murdered. Within several weeks, she killed Davis, his sister Genevieve, and two of his daughters, Minnie and Edna.

The surviving family members ordered a toxicology exam on Davis' daughter, Minnie. The official report discovered that she had been poisoned. A police detail was put on Toppan.

ARREST AND TRIAL

Local authorities arrested her for murder on October 29, 1901. Toppan had confessed to 31 murders by 1902.

In court, Toppan insisted she was sane. She claimed that she could not be insane if she knew what she was doing and knew that it was wrong, but she was declared insane and committed. On June 23, the Barnstable County Courthouse declared her not guilty because of insanity and committed for life in the Taunton Insane Hospital.

OUTCOME

Jane Toppan died on October 29, 1938, at the age of 84.

MEDIA

Jon Keves wrote and directed the independent film "American Nightmare." Debbie Rochon played a serial killer named "Jane Toppan" in this movie.

Jane Toppan was featured in one of six monologues in the play Murderess by Anne Bertram, which premiered in Minnesota, at Theatre Unbound. Mishia Burns Edwards directed the segment "The Truth About Miss Toppan," and Laura Wiebers portrayed her in it.

Toppan was also the subject of an episode of Deadly Women and episodes of the podcasts Criminal, "My Favorite Murder."

- ◊ **Date of birth:** July 1868
- ◊ **Nicknames:** Black Widow
- ◊ **Motive:** Life Insurance Policy
- ◊ **Number of victims:** 9
- ◊ **Date of murders:** 1893 – 1913
- ◊ **Date of arrest:** 1911
- ◊ **Murder method:** Poisoning
- ◊ **Known victims**: Her first husband, Fred Brinkamp; her stepdaughter, 26-year-old Lillian Brinkamp; her second husband Charles Vermilya; her stepson, Harry Vermilya; her 23-year-old stepson from her first marriage, Frank Brinkamp; a railroad fireman, Jason Rupert; her third husband, Richard Smith
- ◊ **Crime location:** Illinois, United States
- ◊ **Status:** Died on December 31, 1913.

BACKGROUND

Louise Vermilya was born in Cook County, Illinois. Her name at birth was Louesa Woolf. Her parents were Prussian immigrants: Wilhemina (née Munaroe) and John Woolf. They had five daughters, and she was the oldest of five girls. On April 2, 1885, Louise married 24-year-old Fred Brinkamp at the age of 16. She moved to the village of Barrington within the Cuba township of Lake County in northern Illinois.

MURDERS

In 1893, Vermilya claimed the life of her first husband, Fred Brinkamp while living on their farm near Barrington, Illinois and the string of homicides began. The coroner stated the cause of Brinkamp's death was a heart attack. Following his death, Vermilya inherited $5,000 from his life insurance policy because he had named her as the beneficiary. No suspicions arose due to Brinkamp's age at death, and it was thought to be due to natural causes. Brinkamp had six children. Two of them met similar fates to their father shortly after his passing away. Cora was the first to die at the age of eight, with her sister Florence following at three and a half.

Undertaker E.N. Blocks owned a mortuary in Barrington. He stated that Louise liked working around bodies. Vermilya seemed to enjoy working in the morgue with Blocks, despite not being a salaried employee.

In 1906, Vermilya moved to Chicago

with her minor charges in tow. Vermilya claimed the life of her stepdaughter, 26-year-old Lillian Brinkamp but the coroner ruled the cause of death as "acute nephritis." The Brinkamp family were thought to be cursed due to the unusually high number of deaths within it.

Around this time, Vermilya remarried a 59-year-old man named Charles Vermilya. Three years later, their marriage ended as he died, apparently victim to a sudden illness. His widow gained $1,000 in cash and a home in Crystal Lake, Illinois. Harry Vermilya died shortly after quarreling with Louise over the sale of the Crystal Lake estate. No suspicions arose after the deaths, and the coincidence was blamed.

In 1910, Frank Brinkamp, Vermilya's 23-year-old son from her first marriage died, and she inherited $1,200 after the death. On his death bed, Frank voiced suspicion involving his stepmother, stating he was going the same way his father did.

Vermilya began poisoning acquaintances. On January 15, 1910, Jason Rupert, a railroad fireman, fell ill after dining with Vermilya. He died in two days but was only the first in a series of deaths in Vermilya's home. Vermilya married a train conductor and boarder at her home, Richard Smith, in February 1910. On March 11, 1910, after eating a meal prepared by Vermilya, he died. The cause of Smith's death was determined to be gastritis. Smith's estranged wife believed that the circumstances surrounding her husband's death were suspicious. Her motive in the deaths of her family members was a pursuit of financial gain. It became unclear after the deaths of her lodgers, for whom she gained no monetary rewards.

ARREST AND TRIAL

Arthur Bissonette and his father came to dine at the Vermilya home in October 1911. While dining with Vermilya, both Bissonettes started suffering abdominal pain. Police detectives became suspicious after questioning Bissonette's father who stated he had seen Vermilya sprinkling "white pepper" over their meals before serving them. The Chicago Police Department did an autopsy on Bissonette's body detecting arsenic poisoning. Soon after the discovery, officials took Vermilya into custody.

Vermilya assisted Bissonette to be accepted into the Home Guard, a militia-like entity for those who were unable to qualify for the military. Bissonette, in return, made a will naming Vermilya as the sole beneficiary of the insurance policy. Bissonette made another will shortly before his death but named his fiancé Lydia Rivard as the beneficiary of his estate. Though he listed Vermilya as the witness, she claimed to not know about ever signing the document.

On November 4, authorities reported Vermilya had been swallowing the "white pepper" since her house arrest on October 28. The officials said she was near her death by November 9. Vermilya suffered valvular heart problems. On November 24, 1911, doctors discharged Vermilya from the county hospital. By December 9, physicians stated she had paralysis, which was a permanent condition.

Vermilya, however, was required to attend all her court proceedings and she did so in a wheelchair. On November 6, 1911, Vermilya was arraigned before Municipal Judge Walker for the death of Arthur Bissonette.

In March 1912, the presiding judge, Judge Kersten, attorney Joseph R. Barres, and the prosecutor on the case had a conference. Professor Walter S. Haines, the Rush Medical College expert chemist, conducted an autopsy and found evidence of arsenic poisoning in Smith's liver. The local officials took Vermilya into custody and she was detained in the county jail where she attempted suicide again. The trial began on 21 March 1912.

Juror selection had become a difficulty as men were unsure whether they could inflict the death penalty on a woman. Vermilya was still in custody awaiting her trial by 12 October 1912. The summer heat in a non-airconditioned jail continued to worsen her health and Vermilya was released on $5,000 bail on 28 June 1913.

On 18 April 1915, the Assistant State's Attorney, Michael Sullivan, and the State Attorney Hoyne held a conference regarding the continuation of the trial. They decided that it would be impossible to obtain a conviction on the Smith indictment without any strong evidence. All charges were dropped per the request of Vermilya's attorney. After the dismissal of her charges, Vermilya led a quiet life as no further documentation of her exists in local papers past this point.

OUTCOME

Louise Vermilya died on December 31, 1913, at the age of 45.

SARAH WHITELING

- ◊ **Date of birth:** 1848
- ◊ **Other names:** The Wholesale Poisoner, The Philadelphia Poisoner, The Philadelphia Murderess
- ◊ **Number of victims:** 3
- ◊ **Date of murders:** March – May 1888
- ◊ **Date of arrest:** November 1888
- ◊ **Murder method:** Poisoning (arsenic)
- ◊ **Known victims**: Her husband, John Whiteling, 38; her daughter, Bertha Whiteling, 9; her son, Willie Whiteling, 2
- ◊ **Crime location:** Pennsylvania, United States
- ◊ **Status:** Executed by hanging

BACKGROUND

Claiming to have been born in Germany, Sarah was initially married to Tom Brown in Clinton, Iowa in 1868. The couple moved to Chicago, but after the Great Fire, they moved to Philadelphia. A few years later, Brown was imprisoned in the Eastern State Penitentiary for highway robbery and died serving his sentence. Sarah then had a child with a man named Thomas Storey, who kept an oyster saloon in the city. In March 1880, she married John Whiteling, bringing along her 9-month-old daughter with them. In 1886, the couple had their child, which they named William C. Whiteling, but nicknamed Willie.

MURDERS

On March 30, 1888, John died suddenly. The attending physician Dr. G. W. Smith evaluated that the cause of death was inflammation of the bowels. His life had been insured in two companies: The John Hancock Financial and the Benevolent Order of Buffalos, each paying Sarah $145 and $85 respectively. When questioned about his death, she claimed that he had committed suicide.

On April 24, Bertha also died, with her verdict being typhoid fever. She, too, had been insured by the John Hancock Financial for $122. And a month after, on May 26, Willie also passed away. Since Dr. Smith abandoned the case, his colleague Dr. Dietrich determined the cause of death as congestion of the bowels. Like his sister and father, he too had been insured: for $30 at the John Hancock Financial, and $17 at Prudential Financial. Sarah refused when asked if the bodies could be examined by the coroner, claiming that when one of her previous children supposedly died in an almshouse, doctors had started the post mortem exam process and realized way too late that the child was still alive.

ARREST, TRIAL, AND EXECUTION

The short intervals of the deaths proved suspicious to Coroner Ashbridge. After an examination with the Health Office, he ordered to investigate the case. With the assistance of Chief Detective Wood and Detective Gyer, the bodies were exhumed from Mechanics' Cemetery. Professor Leffman performed an examination and discovered large amounts of arsenic in the bodies. Sarah Jane Whiteling was arrested shortly after and placed on suicide watch. She spent most of her imprisonment in prayer and suffering from nervous prostration wanting a physician to be called in; she finally gave in and confessed to murdering her two children using "Rough on Rats."

When questioned about her motives, Mrs. Whiteling claimed that she had murdered Bertha to prevent her from becoming a "sinful and wicked girl," as she had misbehaved continuously and stolen various items, such as pennies and pocketbooks, from her teacher and neighbors. As for Willie, she had poisoned him because he was "in the way." However, when it came to John's death, Sarah vehemently denied murdering him and instead claimed that while she indeed did buy the poison, he had taken it by his own volition because of the family's extreme poverty. After the murders, she had planned to take her own life but decided against it since the Bible states that those who take their own life cannot enter Heaven.

At her trial, Whiteling's lawyer tried his best to convince the jury that his client was insane and had to be sentenced to life imprisonment. After deliberating on the issue, however, they returned and pronounced her guilty of the crimes. While the verdict didn't affect Sarah at all, it shocked the contemporary public in Philadelphia, especially the female population, who went so far as to sign a petition for commutation of her sentence. Despite this, Gov. Beaver did not change her sentence, and Whiteling was sentenced to death by hanging for murdering her daughter, as there was insufficient evidence for the other murders. While imprisoned, the officials informed Sarah that she had been left a fortune from a deceased relative back in Iowa.

On the execution date, Sarah Whiteling appeared to be unmoved by her conundrum, as she believed that God would forgive her sins and that she would go to Heaven to be with her children. On June 25, 1889, at 10 o'clock, following a short prayer, the trap was sprung. Whiteling suffocated from strangulation, although, according to physicians, her heart had continued beating for a little while after the drop. The officials then sent her body for dissection to Dr. Alice W. Bennett, who examined her brain, before eventually sending her body off to be buried alongside her murdered relatives.

SHIRLEY WINTERS

◊ **Date of birth:** February 27, 1958
◊ **Nicknames:** Arsonist
◊ **Motive:** Mental health problems
◊ **Number of victims:** 2 – 10
◊ **Date of murders:** November 21, 1980 – November 28, 2006
◊ **Date of arrest:** March 2007
◊ **Murder method:** Suffocation, drowning
◊ **Known victims**: Her 5-month-old son Ronald Winters III, 2-year-old Ryan Rivers
◊ **Crime location:** New York, United States
◊ **Status:** A St. Lawrence County Court judge sentenced her to 20 years in prison on June 16, 2008. An Onondaga County Court judge sentenced her to 8 1/3 to 25 years in prison on June 17, 2008. She serves the sentences at the same time.

BACKGROUND

In 1966, at the age of eight, Winters lost her three siblings: a ten-year-old brother, a four-year-old sister, and an eleven-year-old sister. The cause of their deaths was an apparent carbon monoxide leak in the family home.

In 1979, Winters lost two other children, three-year-old Colleen, and twenty-month-old John in a fire in their family's cabin on Hyde Lake in Theresa, New York. Officials determined the cause of the fire to be an electrical defect. In March 2007, the officials exhumed the bodies of those children. The autopsies showed that both Colleen and John suffered blunt force head injuries before the fire.

There had been a fire in her friend's house in nearby Hermon, New York the previous day. In 2007, St. Lawrence County authorities also re-opened their investigation into that incident.

Since the 1979 fire, Winters has been near 17 fires, nine of which have been determined to be arson. In 1981, she pleaded guilty to criminal mischief about two of the fires, and in 1997 was convicted of arson in another fire, one that burned her mother's home, for which she spent eight years in prison. In 2005, she was released. Winters' mother died in a car accident two months before her prison sentence began.

On November 12, 1989, another of the fires occurred in a home in which Winters was staying in Syracuse with her three children. She rescued her four-year-old daughter and her two-year-old son but lost track of her oldest living child, a five-year-old daughter, who rescued herself.

MURDERS, ARREST, AND TRIAL

On November 28, 2006, Winters visited Ryan Rivers' grandparents. He was found to be drowned at the Pierrepont home where his grandparents lived. In August 2007, St. Lawrence County grand jury indicted Winters of second-degree murder, first-degree assault and endangering the welfare of a child.

The police decided to exhume Winters' son, Ronald Winters III. Doctors supposed he died of Sudden Infant Death Syndrome on November 21, 1980. On March 28, 2007, based on their findings, police charged Winters with second-degree murder.

Winters pleaded guilty for drowning Rivers on April 21, 2008. In Onondaga County Court she also agreed to plead guilty for smothering Winters. The authorities sentenced her to twenty years for Rivers, and eight to twenty-five years for Winters with parole eligibility after 17 years. Winters is imprisoned at Bedford Hills Correctional Facility. By pleading guilty, she avoided possible second-degree murder convictions and multiple life sentences. Winters also avoided her prosecution for the 1979 murders of Colleen and John Winters.

MEDIA

Winters' many crimes were featured on episode 8: "A Trail of Ashes & Bodies in Otisco, New York" of the podcast Small Town Murder.

A book, published under the title Teflon Shelly and written by Ron Ryan, closely resembles the case and investigation into Winters.

OUTCOME

A St. Lawrence County Court judge sentenced her to 20 years in prison on June 16, 2008. An Onondaga County Court judge sentenced her to 8 1/3 to 25 years in prison on June 17, 2008. She serves the sentences at the same time.

MARTHA WISE

- ◊ **Date of birth:** 1884
- ◊ **Nicknames:** The Borgia of America
- ◊ **Number of victims:** 3 killed and 14 injured
- ◊ **Date of murders:** 1924 – 1925
- ◊ **Date of arrest:** 1925
- ◊ **Murder method:** Poisoning (arsenic)
- ◊ **Known victims:** Her mother, Sophie Hasel; her aunt, Lily Gienke
- ◊ **Crime location:** Ohio, United States
- ◊ **Status:** In May 1925, sentenced to life in prison. Died in prison on June 28, 1971.

BACKGROUND

Martha Wise was born Martha Hasel in 1884 in Hardscrabble, Ohio, to Sophie Hasel and her husband, both of whom were farmers. The family also had three sons and one more daughter, although contemporary sources name only one of Martha's siblings, a brother named Fred. In 1906, Martha met Albert Wise who was substantially older. They were married, though Wise refused to give her a wedding ring.

The marriage was unhappy. Martha moved onto his 50-acre (20 ha) farm but quickly found out that Albert expected a farmhand more than a wife. She was forced to do farm work even when pregnant. Her work was generally male-oriented. At the same time, nobody released her from the usual household chores of cleaning and baking. Their first child, Albert, did not survive infancy; four others, Everett, Gertrude, Kenneth, and Lester, did.

Martha seldom missed a visit to any funeral held in or near Hardscrabble. It was her main source of diversion. When asked, she said that she liked funerals. In 1923, Albert Wise died. He left his wife a 40-year-old widow with four children. People noticed her odd behavior and fixation on funerals as she not only attended funerals but openly cried at them, no matter who had died.

MURDERS

Soon after Albert's death, Martha found new male companionship, Walter Johns. He worked as a farmhand on property near her farm. The Hasel family viewed the relationship with disfavor. Both her mother and her aunt, Lily Gienke, wanted Martha to end the relationship with Walter. In 1924, Martha consented, and the relationship ended. He moved to Cleveland, and the couple lost contact.

On Thanksgiving Day, 1924, several members of Martha's family, including her mother, fell ill with severe stomach complaints. The others recovered shortly, but her mother's illness worsened, and she died on December 13, 1924. New Year's Eve brought more disease. Lily Gienke, her husband Fred, and some of their children began suffering stomach pains like those Martha's mother, Sophie, had experienced before death. Several family members were hospitalized, and by February 1925, Lily and Fred were both dead. In the fall and winter of 1924 – 1925, seventeen relatives were taken ill with similar symptoms. Four of the Gienke children were partially paralyzed from the mysterious illness.

ARREST AND TRIAL

After the deaths of the Gienkes, officials began to investigate their deaths. The county sheriff, Fred Roshon, soon learned that Martha had purchased large quantities of arsenic at a local drug store. Lily's autopsy confirmed the presence of arsenic in her digestive tract. When questioned by the sheriff, Martha claimed she had bought the arsenic to kill rats. Later she confessed that she had used it to poison family members. Martha put it in water buckets and coffee pots the family drank out of.

On March 23, 1925, despite her confession, Martha pleaded not guilty to the charge of murdering Lily in front of a grand jury. Martha told that she was overwhelmingly attracted to attending funerals, and when there were not enough funerals in the community, she created them by killing. Martha was indicted of first-degree murder on April 7, 1925.

On May 4, 1925, the authorities began Martha's trial for murder. Her lawyer was Joseph Pritchard, and the prosecutor was Joseph Seymour. The defense stated that Wise was insane and that her former lover, Walter Johns, ordered her to commit the murders. Martha's sister-in-law, Edith Hasel, and her husband Fred Hasel wanted to testify for the defense, but on May 6, Edith committed suicide. Three of the Gienkes' children and Martha's son, Lester, testified against her.

The jury found Martha guilty of first-degree murder. The judge sentenced Martha to life imprisonment, under the terms of which only executive clemency could set her free.

OUTCOME

In 1962, Governor Michael DiSalle commuted her sentence to second-degree murder because of Martha's good behavior in prison. At the age of 79, she was paroled. Martha's family refused to take her in, and several rest homes for the elderly also declined her residency. Martha returned to prison. The officials revoked her parole and the commutation of her sentence. She died in jail on June 28, 1971.

MEDIA

In 1930, Toledo News-Bee article series featured Martha Wise. In 1962, St. Joseph Gazette called her case "one of Ohio's most publicized crimes of the era," and labeled her the "poison widow of Hardscrabble." In 2008, the episode of the Investigation Discovery series Deadly Women also covered Wise's case.

AILEEN WUORNOS

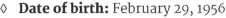

- ◊ **Date of birth:** February 29, 1956
- ◊ **Other names:** Susan Lynn Blahovec, Sandra Kretsch, Lee Blahovec, Cammie Marsh Greene, Lori Kristine Grody
- ◊ **Motive:** Hated humans for a long time
- ◊ **Number of victims:** 7
- ◊ **Date of murders:** November 30, 1989 - November 19, 1990
- ◊ **Date of arrest:** January 9, 1991
- ◊ **Murder method:** Shooting
- ◊ **Known victims:** Richard Mallory, age 51; David Spears, age 43; Charles Carskaddon, age 40; Peter Siems, age 65; Troy Burress, age 50; Charles "Dick" Humphreys, age 56; Walter Jeno Antonio, age 62.
- ◊ **Crime location:** Florida, United States
- ◊ **Status:** On October 9, 2002, executed by lethal injection in Florida.

BACKGROUND

Aileen Wuornos was born in February 1956, in Michigan. Her name at birth was Aileen Carol Pittman. Her mother, Diane Wuornos, was Finnish-American. She was 14 years old when on June 3, 1954, she married Aileen's father, Leo Dale Pittman, who was 16 at the time.

Aileen had an older brother Keith who was born on March 14, 1955. She never met her father because two months before her birth, her mother, Diane, filed for divorce.

Wuornos' father was incarcerated at the time she was born. Doctors diagnosed Leo Dale Pittman with schizophrenia. Later officials convicted him of sex crimes against children. On January 30, 1969, he committed suicide by hanging in prison. In January 1960, Diane abandoned her children. Wuornos was almost four years old. Her mother left children with their maternal grandparents, Lauri, and Britta Wuornos. On March 18, 1960, they legally adopted Keith and Aileen.

Eleven-year-old Wuornos started engaging in sexual activities in school in exchange for drugs, cigarettes, and food. She also had sexual activities with her brother. Aileen's grandfather was an alcoholic, and she claimed that he had sexually assaulted her when she was a child. He also beat her, and before beating, he would force her to take off her clothes. In 1970, at the age of 13, she

became pregnant, having been raped by an accomplice of her grandfather. On March 23, 1971, Wuornos gave birth to a boy at a home for unwed mothers. She placed the child for adoption. Aileen dropped out of school a few months after her son was born. At about the same time, her grandmother died. Grandfather threw 15-year-old Wuornos out of the house, and she lived in the woods near her old home and supported herself as a prostitute.

On May 27, 1974, 18-year-old Wuornos was arrested in Jefferson County, Colorado. She was driving under the influence and firing a .22-caliber pistol from a moving car.

In 1976, Wuornos met 69-year-old yacht club President Lewis Gratz Fell in Florida. They married quickly, and the reporters printed the announcement in the local newspaper. At the local bar, Wuornos involved herself in confrontations and went to jail for assault. She also hit Fell with his cane, leading him to gain a restraining order against her within weeks of the marriage. She returned to Michigan, and on July 14, 1976, the officials arrested her in Antrim County and charged with assault. Her brother Keith died of cancer on July 17, and Wuornos received $10,000 from his life insurance. On July 21 after only nine weeks, Wuornos and Fell annulled their marriage. Within two months, Wuornos spent the money inherited from her brother. She bought a new car and wrecked it shortly afterward.

In May 1981, the police arrested Wuornos for the armed robbery of a store in Edgewater, Florida. She stole two packs of cigarettes and $35. On May 4, 1982, she was sentenced to prison, and released on June 30, 1983. The officials arrested Wuornos again on May 1, 1984. She tried to pass forged checks at a bank in Key West. On January 4, 1986, the police arrested Wuornos in Miami and charged her with car theft. Miami police officers found a box of ammunition and a .38-caliber revolver and in the stolen car. On June 2, 1986, deputy sheriffs questioned Wuornos for pulling a gun in a male companion's car and demanding $200. They found Wuornos to be carrying spare ammunition, and police discovered a .22 pistol under the passenger seat she had occupied.

In 1986, Wuornos met a hotel maid, Tyria Moore, at a Daytona Beach gay bar. As they moved in together, Wuornos sold her earnings to support them. On July 4, 1987, Daytona Beach police questioned Wuornos and Moore at a bar for an incident in which the police accused them of assault and beating with a beer bottle. Wuornos blamed a Daytona Beach bus driver of an attack on March 12, 1988. She asserted that he pushed her off the bus. The police listed Moore as a witness to the incident. Up until her execution, Wuornos claimed to still be in love with Moore.

MURDERS

W uornos killed seven men within twelve months.

On November 30, 1989, she killed 51-year-old Richard Mallory, who was an electronics store owner in Clearwater. Wuornos claimed to have killed her first victim in self-defense. A deputy sheriff found Mallory's abandoned vehicle two days later. The officials found Richard's body several miles away in a wooded area on December 13. Wuornos had shot him. The cause of death was two bullets in the left lung.

Forty-three-year-old David Spears, a construction worker in Winter Garden was Wuornos' second victim. She had shot him six times. The police found his naked body along Florida State Road 19 in Citrus County on June 1, 1990.

She murdered a 40-year-old part-time rodeo worker, Charles Carskaddon, on May 31, 1990. The officials found his body in Pasco County on June 6, 1990. Wuornos had shot him nine times with a small-caliber weapon.

A 65-year-old retired merchant seaman, Peter Siems, devoted much of his time to a Christian outreach ministry. In June 1990, Siems left Florida for Arkansas. The police officers found his car in Orange Springs, Florida, on July 4, 1990, but his body was never found. Somebody had seen Moore and Wuornos abandoning the vehicle, and the experts found Wuornos' palm print on the interior door handle.

Wuornos murdered a 50-year-old sausage salesman, Troy Burress, from Ocala. The officials reported him missing on July 31, 1990. The police officers found his body on August 4, 1990, in a wooded area along State Road 19 in Marion County. He had been shot twice.

The body of 56-year-old Charles "Dick" Humphreys was found in Marion County on September 11, 1990. He was a retired U.S. Air Force Major, former State Child Abuse Investigator, and former Chief of Police. Wuornos killed him on September 12, 1990 by shooting him six times.

A 62-year-old security guard, trucker, and police reservist, Walter Jeno Antonio, was Wuornos' last victim. His almost naked body was found near a remote logging road in Dixie County on November 19, 1990. She had shot him four times.

ARREST AND TRIAL

On January 9, 1991, the police arrested Wuornos at The Last Resort, a biker bar in Volusia County. The next day, the police officers found Moore in Scranton, Pennsylvania. She agreed to provoke a confession from Wuornos in exchange for inviolability from prosecution. She made numerous telephone calls to Wuornos under police guidance. She pleaded for help in clearing her name. Wuornos confessed to the murders on January 16, 1991. She claimed the men had tried to abuse her and she killed them in self-defense.

Wuornos went to trial for the killing of Mallory on January 14, 1992. With help from Moore's testimony, the officials convicted Wuornos of Mallory's murder on January 27, 1992. Psychiatrists for the defense stated that Wuornos was mentally unstable. They had diagnosed her with an antisocial and borderline personality disorder. On February 1, the judge sentenced her to death.

On March 31, 1992, Wuornos pleaded no dispute to the murders of Humphreys, Spears, and Burress. Wuornos was given three more death sentences on May 15, 1992.

Wuornos received her fifth death sentence for the murder of Carskaddon in November 1992.

Aileen Wuornos pleaded guilty to the murder of Walter Jeno Antonio, and in February 1993, she was sentenced to death again. In all, she received six death sentences.

EXECUTION

Wuornos was placed at the Florida Department of Corrections Broward Correctional Institution death row for women. Then she was transferred to the Florida State Prison for execution. In 1996, the U.S. Supreme Court denied her appeal.

In 2002, Wuornos began accusing the prison staff of tainting her food with saliva, dirt, and urine.

Before the execution, Wuornos gave a series of interviews to a filmmaker Nick Broomfield.

Wuornos' execution took place on October 9, 2002. She died at 9:47 a.m. She rejected her last meal and opted for a cup of coffee instead. Before death, Wuornos said she was sailing with the rock and would be back, like Independence Day, with Jesus.

Wuornos's body was cremated, and the ashes were spread beneath a tree in her native Michigan.

BOOKS

Journalist Sue Russell wrote a book Lethal Intent about Wuornos in 2002. In 2012, Lisa Kester and Daphne Gottlieb published the book titled Dear Dawn: Aileen Wuornos in Her Own Words, which is a collection of letters written by Wuornos over ten years.

MEDIA

Nick Broomfield directed two documentaries about Wuornos: in 1993, Aileen Wuornos: The Selling of a Serial Killer, and in 2003, Aileen: Life and Death of a Serial Killer.

Wuornos was featured in the episodes of the documentary TV series American Justice, Biography and Deadly Women. An episode of the TV series The New Detectives also tells about her.

The Reelz Television Network chronicled the case in an episode of Murder Made Me Famous which was aired December 1, 2018.

In 1992, Jean Smart starred as Aileen in the TV movie Overkill: The Aileen Wuornos Story.

Charlize Theron starred as Wuornos in the theatrical film Monster in 2003.

SEE ALSO OUR COLORING BOOK

THAT PERFECTLY COMPLEMENTS THIS BOOK:

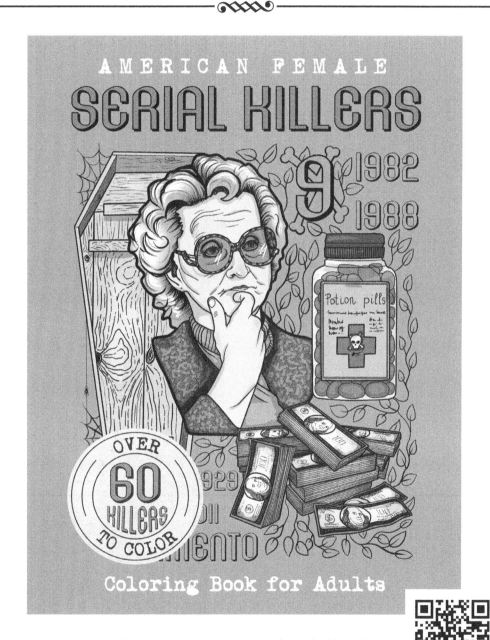

https://www.amazon.com/dp/9526925548

Made in the USA
Las Vegas, NV
30 January 2023

66526183R00083